BACHELOR 101:
Cooking + Cleaning = Closing

BACHELOR 101:
COOKING + CLEANING = CLOSING
JAMIE REIDY

Copyright © 2009 by Jamie Reidy
ISBN 978-0-578-03463-8

CONTENTS

INTRODUCTION IX
PART ONE: FOOD 1
   THE RULES 2
   KITCHEN ESSENTIALS 3
   FLAVOR ESSENTIALS 4
   APPETIZERS
       SARAH'S "EVER READY" APPETIZER 5
       AMBER'S CAPRESE SALAD 6
       SUSAN'S CRAB CAKES 7
   SALADS
       DARREN'S ONE-MINUTE SALAD 10
       CHEF ZACH'S ARUGULA SALAD 11
       JAMIE'S LETTUCE-LESS SALAD 12
   BEEF
       JERRY'S ROUND STEAK 15
       JAMIE'S' BROILED RIBEYE STEAK 17
       JAMIE'S SPICY MEATLOAF 20
   POULTRY
       BARTON'S RUSSIAN CHICKEN 25
       CURT'S CRUMBY CHICKEN 27
       SUSAN'S WORLD'S GREATEST CHICKEN 30
       MONICA'S CHICKEN PARM 33
       EMILY'S "SEAL THE DEAL" CHICKEN 36
       THREE COOKS' CHICKEN DIVAN TO DIE FOR 39
       JONES'S BAKED CHICKEN WITH ONION RINGS 42
       LAURENCE'S "LOVE CHICKEN" 45
       KLEIMAN'S ROSEMARY BREWED CHICKEN 50
       SYNOR'S BLACK BEAN CHICKEN CHILI 54
       PRANSKY'S TURKEY PICATTA 57

PORK
- AMMO'S HONEY-MUSTARD PORK CHOPS ... 62
- STEVE'S "EASY PORK" TENDERLOIN ... 64

SEAFOOD
- SUZY'S BAKED SALMON ... 68
- CHEF ZACH'S LEMON-CAPER SWORDFISH & ARUGULA SALAD ... 71
- JOHANNA'S BASIL SHRIMP ... 74
- BRENT'S SHRIMP SCAMPI ... 78

PASTA & PIZZA
- "JUST WHAT THE DOCTOR ORDERED" PASTA ... 81
- JB'S SALSA SPAGHETTI ... 84
- EJ'S "REVERSE COWBOY" BARBEQUE CHICKEN PIZZA ... 86
- MARISA'S MEXICAN LASAGNA ... 88
- CHEF ZACH'S LASAGNA BOLOGNESE ... 92

COMMIE PINKO, ER, VEGETARIAN ENTREES
- AMMO'S 6-CAN VEGGIE CHILI ... 97
- BRENT'S VEGGIE PASTA ... 101

VEGGIE SIDES
- KAYCE'S RASPBERRY VINAIGRETTE ASPARAGUS ... 104
- GRETCHEN'S LEMON-BASIL CARROTS ... 105

STARCHY SIDES
- CURT'S BAKED POTATOES IN THE MICROWAVE ... 108
- POEPPE'S PARTY POTATOES ... 109

DESSERT
- DESSERT ... 113

BREAKFAST
- JIMMY O'S BREAKFAST BURRITO ... 114

PART TWO: ABODE ... 117
- GETTING STARTED ... 118
- CLEANING ESSENTIALS ... 119
- ON THE WAY IN ... 120
- KITCHEN ... 121

- LIVING ROOM 125
- BATHROOM 129
- BEDROOM 135

PART THREE: DUDE **138**
- PRE-FLIGHT CHECKLIST 139
- PRE-SHOWER 140
- IN SHOWER 141
- POST-SHOWER 142
- POST-DRESSING 143

AFTERWORD **144**

ACKNOWLEDGMENTS **145**

INTRODUCTION

The Who (Not the band):

Consider You.

You're a bachelor who eats out or orders takeout more often than not. You microwave leftovers or frozen dinners on the other nights. When friends invite you to dinner, they ask you to bring chips and salsa. Maybe.

You never cook because you can't cook and you can't cook because you're afraid to cook. Sound familiar?

I was You until February 2007, when I started to write this book.

The Why:

There are two undeniably practical reasons for you to learn to cook: it's healthier and it's cheaper. But I know you don't care about the former; in fact, it probably pushes you even further from the kitchen. The latter might get you to consider cooking, but it's not gonna seal the deal.

But what if I told you, "Women love men who cook"? Winner Winner, chicken dinner!

Hey, don't take my word for it. Listen to Melissa Haro, one of the 2008 "Sports Illustrated" swimsuit models. The magazine asked her, "What's the sexiest thing a man has ever done for you?" The stunning brunette replied, "Cook. I love a man who can cook."

Your Honor…the Defense rests.

Picture this: You meet Susie at a Happy Hour (you're there for the free taco bar). You chat. You flirt. You ask for her number and then punch it right into your cell phone. Maybe you even take a picture, so you can place the name with the face by the time you get around to calling three days later. You ask Susie to dinner.

You choose this option because it is traditional and easy.

But the dinner date is also problematic, for three important reasons. First, regardless of the restaurant you pick, Susie has probably already been there. Maybe she had a terrible experience the last time she was there – scene of a breakup? Maybe she had an amazing time with a guy for whom she still pines. Either way, Susie is going to be distracted, and distracted ≠ horny. Secondly, you may not know a Pinot Grigio from a Pinot Noir. If Susie knows anything about wine or fine food, you are going to feel silly, a quality that won't inspire her desire or your confidence. Lastly, you may not have the coin to finance an expensive culinary expedition. God forbid some rich dude wined and dined Susie recently; your weak effort (Blake let me order salad and an appetizer!) will clinch an early night.

Looking irrelevant, foolish and/or cheap…not exactly the Triple Crown you're going for. I'm offering you a much more palatable alternative: Invite Susie over for a home-cooked meal.

Any guy can take her to dinner. No guy has made her dinner.

The What:

This book won't make you the next Naked Chef, but it can make you the next chef to get naked.

Bachelor 101 gives you 27 simple, step-by-step recipes that even a kitchen-phobe can ace. I'm not talking "haute cuisine," here. In fact, I'm not even sure what "haute cuisine" means. I'm talking dinner: a protein, a carb and a veggie (Note: I consider salad to be a perfectly acceptable veggie; after all, it's mostly green. But, if you insist on making a side veggie dish in addition to salad, dude, I've provided three recipes).

Now, repeat after me: Presentation Schmesentation. You will not "drizzle" chocolate or raspberry or anything else in pretty patterns. You will not construct a food tower that will come crashing down the first time a fork touches it. Chicken + Microwavable Rice + Bag of pre-washed Salad = Dinner.

And here's the kicker: even if you burn the chicken, you will have scored major points for trying! In fact, burning the chicken might just be a good thing, as you'll appear vulnerable, and women love vulnerability. Besides, you'll still have plenty of wine and bread and salad to sustain the two of you, as well as something to laugh about.

Basically, there is no downside to cooking for Susie.

The How:

If you're anything like me, you're going to be scared shitless the first time you try to cook. Fortunately for you, I've asked all the questions and made all the mistakes so that you won't have to do either.

What pots and pans does a bachelor absolutely need to have? What seasonings are a must? Bachelor 101 answers these and more. I provide you with checklists you can rip out and take into Target; Bed, Bath and Beyond; or the supermarket.

I explain what wines to offer with each meal. More importantly, I explain where the wine glass goes on the table. Which one's the "fish fork?" The more appropriate question is, "Who cares?" You will not be cooking any meals that require more than a salad fork and a, uh, regular fork.

I have pressed weights, shirts and my luck, but I have never pressed garlic. And neither will you. Every ingredient can be purchased in a box, bag, can or jar. Mixing is kept to a minimum. If you ever have more than two pans/pots going at once, something is wrong.

I took notes throughout every step of the cooking process: at the supermarket (price, location of items), during preparation (degree of difficulty, precise amount of time necessary, potential pitfalls), and during serving (is it messy getting it on the plate?). All that information is provided for each recipe, in a clueless man's "Zagat's" format. Only, in Bachelor 101 each recipe is rated according to its easiness (between 1-4 "Chefs," with 1 being the least difficult) and cheapness (approximate dollar amount, which will seem expensive because it includes the price of all the seasonings, etc. I assumed that, like me, you wouldn't actually buy them in advance). This way, you can decide what to cook based upon your confidence and your cash flow.

Once I decided to learn how to cook some basic meals, I solicited recipes from dozens of women with the following guidance: If your 22-year old brother called you in a panic and said he'd met a girl at a bar while watching college football and – running his mouth – promised to cook her dinner tonight, only he doesn't have any idea how to cook and she's gonna be there in three hours… what recipe would you give him?

After weeding through more than 150 submissions, I sought professional help. Chef Zach McGowan, who has appeared on the Food Network's "2 Dudes Catering," contributed three recipes. David LeFevre, executive chef at Los Angeles' Water Grill, gave me tips on seasonings and advice for how to prepare red meat. Mike Simms, former general manager of Napa Valley's Tra Vigne restaurant and current creator/owner of the Tin Roof Bistro, provided the wine recommendations that accompany each entree.

I personally tested each recipe to ensure they are You-proof. None of them were! I learned that women are born with brains pre-programmed to decode recipes. Male brains...not so much.

When I tried to follow the recipes, I struggled to make sense of the paragraph formats. To alleviate confusion, I've numbered each specific step, making it easy for you to follow along and keep your place. Why should you have to remember that "T" means "tablespoon", while "t" means "teaspoon?" I spell them out – TABLEspoon and TEAspoon – so there's no knowledge required. Lastly, the recipes provide the utensils and cookware you'll be using in the order you'll be using them.

My hands-on trial by fire – thankfully, that's still just a figure of speech in my kitchen – allowed me to provide humorous, yet helpful insights that never would have occurred to an experienced cook.

For example, the Turkey Picatta recipe calls for two tablespoons of butter. When I first read that direction, I asked myself, "How do I measure a tablespoon of butter? I mean, shouldn't it be a tableknife?" But then I unwrapped the stick of butter...and saw a RULER on the wax paper. Some Merlin of Measurement had already thought of this, brother! So, in my instructions I explain that you need to line up your knife with the appropriate mark on the wrapper, and slice off your two tablespoons of butter.

Each recipe contains hints to avoid mistakes I made – "Don't drop the TURKEY CUTLETS into the boiling OIL. SPLAT! OUCH! Gently lay CUTLETS in the skillet." – and elementary explanations of all cooking directions.

Another thing I learned? Cooking is fun. I can't believe I just typed those words, but I shit you not. These days, I cook 2-3 times per week.

The What Else:

Okay, Romeo, so Susie is ready to come over for dinner. Is your place ready for Susie?

When I started writing Bachelor 101, I looked around my one-bedroom beach pad and asked myself, "If I wanted to impress a woman tonight...what would I do differently?" The answer bummed me out. Everything. I had no idea I was such a slob! How I ever got a girl to come back a second time I do not know.

Objectively assessing my living space for the first time, I identified innumerable problem areas...and easy ways to fix them. More importantly, I wrote them all down. Then, I asked 80 single women to email me their "deal breakers," things in a guy's apartment that they would instantly find repulsive. You will reap the benefits of their warnings. I even give you a checklist of the cleaning products necessary to get the apartment sparkling.

But I don't stop with the bachelor pad; I spell out ways to get the bachelor looking good, too. Just as a pilot goes through a Pre-flight checklist every time he flies, you need to examine yourself prior to every date. I have provided pre and post-shower routines to ensure you are ready for takeoff. Nose hairs? Backne? Brown weave belt? I've got you covered.

The Wrap:

By following the directions in Bachelor 101, you will be able to dazzle women on Date Nights and inexpensively feed yourself on Off Nights.

Ready to pre-heat that oven?

PART ONE: FOOD

THE RULES

- Wash your hands before cooking. Do not dry them on your jeans!
- Do not cook and/or clean in the shirt you're gonna wear on the date. If you insist on doing so, then at least get one of your Dad's old button-downs to use as a smock, just like in second grade art class.
- Speaking of cleaning, you're gonna make a mess when you cook. This is an irrefutable fact and there's nothing you can do about it. So don't get pissed. As long as the kitchen was clean before you started cooking, you're all good.
- Drink up. Wine, beer, whatever. Cooking is a universally acceptable excuse to imbibe, sort of like Halloween is a universally acceptable excuse for women to dress slutty. I don't know why that is, but the reason is irrelevant. Let's just embrace the fact that the world lets rookie chefs "take the edge off." That said, slurring before the appetizer isn't cute, so try not to kill a bottle of red before Ms. Right Now arrives.
- Crank the tunes! Cooking is gonna be fun, remember?
- If something doesn't smell right, open the kitchen window and hit the exhaust fan immediately.
- You need some info before you cook for her:

Is there anything she doesn't eat? Anything. You have to grill her on this – pardon the pun – to avoid her arriving and declaring her deep-rooted hatred of tomatoes. Which reminds me…

Is she allergic to anything? Even if she says "no," be safe and buy some Benadryl (an antihistamine to treat hives), just in case.

How does she like her steak: rare, medium, well done? If it's the latter, you might consider canceling.

Pregnant women should avoid fish, so keep that in mind. Of course, if you're cooking for a woman who was pregnant when you asked her out, that raises other issues.

KITCHEN ESSENTIALS

- 8" Chef's knife (You might want to buy two of these, just in case Ms. Right Now ever helps you chop, dice, whatever)
- 9" non-stick Frying pan
- Two-gallon pot (pasta, chili, etc.)
- One-quart pot (soups, sauces, etc.)
- Glass cooking Dish (lasagna size)
- Casserole Dish (half the size of the lasagna dish)
- Cookie sheet (btw, if you're short on storage space, the oven – a turned off oven – is a great place to keep the cookie sheet, one-quart pots, etc.
- Wood cutting board
- Oven Mitts – 2
- Colorful mixing/salad bowl (If you get a colorful one, you can use it for both. Otherwise, you need two separate ones)
- Tongs for tossing salad, picking up spaghetti, etc.
- Colander (strainer type thing) to drain pasta, salad, edamame (soy beans, a common appetizer at Sushi restaurants and an easy, healthy snack at home)
- Wooden spoon
- Liquid Measuring Cup
- Measuring Spoons (you know, the ones your mom has; they're connected like Doc Ock)
- Peeler (for, uh, peeling potatoes, carrots, etc.)
- Fish Spatula (this is the best spatula around, and can be used on everything from eggs to steak to fish to grilled cheese)
- Ladle
- Wrappers: Saran Wrap, 2-gallon plastic freezer bags and aluminum foil.
- Instant-Read Meat thermometer
- Baster (This is the huge eye-dropper that you use to re-apply juices to a roast, etc.)
- Basting Brush (You'd use this to directly apply melted butter, ranch dressing etc.)
- Dependable corkscrew (Practice with it so you don't look like a tool in front of her!)
- Matching Wine Glasses; 2. Should be four, but I'll let you slide.
- Fire Extinguisher (I'm just saying)

FLAVOR ESSENTIALS

You can stockpile your seasonings a few different ways:
1) You can ask your mom, aunt or sister to buy you a ready-made spice rack (This is the method recommended by most experts).
2) You can rip out this list and take it into the supermarket to buy everything that you need (Not a bad choice, but more expensive than option #1).
3) You can buy them piecemeal, i.e. get what you need for a particular meal when you need it.

I chose option #3. I wish I'd picked either of the other two! Trust me, it's a royal pain in the ass to have to run out to the supermarket at the last minute because you forgot to buy dried Rosemary flakes earlier that day.

It may seem like a lot of money to shell out up front (spices generally run $6 per bottle or jar), but it's worth the time and hassle saved.

Remember: if the approximate dollar amount for each recipe seems really expensive, it's only because the cost includes all the seasonings required. So, if you buy them all in advance (or get someone else to do so!), the meals themselves will be considerably cheaper.

- Sea Salt (Chef Zach says you must use sea salt or Kosher salt)
- Black Pepper
- Extra Virgin Olive Oil
- Butter (Yes, you're right. Butter isn't technically a "seasoning." But I didn't know where else to include it, and you'll be using it a lot.)
- Garlic Powder
- Balsamic Vinegar
- Cayenne Pepper
- Basil Flakes
- Oregano
- Mrs. Dash
- Chili Powder
- Rosemary Flakes
- Basil Flakes
- Sage Flakes

APPETIZERS

Sarah's "Ever Ready" Appetizer

My cousin Sarah (Reidy) Ferguson flips houses like you flip burgers. And when she's not wowing her husband and friends with her interior design skills, she's blowing them away with her culinary creations.

This appetizer is pretty much ALWAYS ready. Just add bread.

Ease: 1 Chef
Cost: $34
Preparation Time: 5 minutes
Cooking Time: Zero.
Ingredients:
Parmesan Cheese – 1 block (keeps well in the fridge for a long time); $3.99
Hard Salami – 1 (also lasts long in the fridge); $6.99
Black Olives – 1 Can (no jars, for some reason); $2.99
Green Olives – 1 Jar; $1.99
Artichoke Hearts – 1 Can; $3.19
Water Crackers – 1 Box; $1.99
Extra Virgin Olive Oil – 1/3 Cup; $6-13
Sea Salt; $3.99
Pepper; $1.99

Tools, etc:
Cutting Board or Serving Platter
Spoon
Knife
Bowl
Small Plate - 2

Directions:
1. Unwrap SALAMI and PARMESAN CHEESE.
2. Place SALAMI and PARMESAN CHEESE on the cutting board/serving platter.
3. Open can of BLACK OLIVES.
4. Spoon 10 BLACK OLIVES onto small plate #1.
5. Open jar of GREEN OLIVES.
6. Spoon 10 GREEN OLIVES onto small plate #1.
7. Spoon 20 ARTICHOKE HEARTS onto small plate #2.

8. Place plates on platter.
9. Open CRACKERS. Add 1 sleeve of CRACKERS to platter. Throw out wrapper.
10. Measure 1/3 Cup of OLIVE OIL and pour into the bowl for dipping.
11. Carry platter, bowl and knife to living room. Bring SALT and PEPPER.
12. The Appetizer is served!

Amber's Caprese Salad

Amber Vacha is a rocking chick. This Minnesota native and beach volleyball babe has season tickets to the Los Angeles Kings hockey team.
Amber warns, "Even if the guy doesn't like balsamic, he needs to fake it because all women love balsamic!" So suck it up.

Ease: 1.5 Chefs
Cost: $18
Preparation Time: 10 minutes
Cooking Time: Zero

Ingredients:
Fresh Buffalo Mozzarella Cheese – 1 pound; $5.99. (Here's a little culinary Etymology: "Buffalo Mozzarella" doesn't get its name from American Bison, but from Water Buffaloes. Italians used the milk of the water buffalo to make their cheese.)
Fresh Basil – $2.99
Tomatoes – 2; $2.99 per pound
Balsamic Vinegar – ¼ cup; $6-13 per bottle
Cracked Black Pepper – 1 TEAspoon; $2.19 per bottle
French Baguette; $1.29

Tools, etc:
Paper Towels
Paring Knife
Cutting Board
Colander (the thingy with all the holes; it's for draining stuff)
Large Plate or Decorative Plate
Measuring Cup
Measuring Spoons

Directions:
1. Wash TOMATOES. Dry them with paper towels.
2. On cutting board, slice TOMATOES into slices ½ inch thick.
3. Place colander in sink.
4. Rinse ICKY GREEN SEEDS off TOMATOES. Drop TOMATOES in colander to dry.

5. Slice MOZZARELLA into slices @ ½ inch thick.
6. Place TOMATO SLICES onto large plate.
7. Place MOZZARELLA SLICES on top of TOMATO SLICES.
8. Cut BASIL into thin STRIPS.
9. Sprinkle BASIL STRIPS on top of MOZZARELLA.
10. Measure ¼ TEAspoon of BALSAMIC VINEGAR and pour 3 lines on one TOMATO/CHEESE/BASIL.
11. Repeat step 10 for each remaining TOMATO/CHEESE/BASIL.
12. Grab CRACKED PEPPER. Twist 2 times above each slice.
13. Cut 4 slices of FRENCH BREAD. Add BREAD to large plate.
14. Carry large plate to table.
15. The Appetizer is served!

Susan's Crab Cakes

Susan Green is a marketing whiz and a kitchen ninja. She can drink you under the table and she looks mighty fine in a pair of shorts on the flag football field.
This appetizer could actually be a meal, as it serves 6.

Ease: 2 Chefs
Cost: $65
Preparation Time: 10 minutes
Cooking Time: 6 minutes

Ingredients:
Refrigerated Dungeness Crab Meat – sixteen ounces; $25.99
Herb Seasoned Stuffing – 1.5 Cups "divided"; $2.99 ("Divided" means the ingredient will be used at different steps in the process. Btw, you have to look very carefully for this; took me a long time to find, even though it's kept in the Stuffing aisle.)
Dried Parsley Flakes – 1 TEAspoon; $2.39
Eggs – 2; $3.69 per dozen
Mayonnaise – 1/3 Cup; $3.00
Dijon Mustard – 2 TEAspoons; $5.69
Worcestershire Sauce – 1 TEAspoon; $2.59 per 5-ounce bottle
Old Bay Seasoning – 2 TEAspoons; $3.29
Tabasco Sauce – 1 TEAspoon; $2.00
Apple – 1 Chopped; $1.99 per pound
Butter – 2 TABLEspoons; $5.50 per package of four sticks
Lemon – 2; $1 per lemon

Wine Recommendation: Chardonnay or, if feeling adventurous, Beaujolais (a.k.a. the French "Two-Buck Chuck")

Tools, etc:
Colander (the thingy with all the holes; it's for draining stuff)
Large Mixing Bowl
Bowl – 2
Measuring Cup
Measuring Spoons
Paring Knife
Wooden Spoon
Large Plate – 2
Large Frying Pan
Paper Towels
Fork
Spatula

Directions:

1. Place colander in sink.
2. Pour 16-ounces of CRAB MEAT into colander to drain.
3. Measure ½ Cup of HERB SEASONED STUFFING and pour into bowl #1.
4. Use a fist, ice cream scooper, spoon, or whatever to crush the STUFFING in the bowl.
5. Measure 1 Cup of HERB SEASONED STUFFING and add to large mixing bowl.
6. Measure 1 TEAspoon of PARSLEY FLAKES and add to large mixing bowl.
7. Measure 1/3 Cup of MAYONNAISE and add to large mixing bowl.
8. Crack 2 EGGS into bowl #2.
9. Use fork to beat EGGS until they are of one consistency and color.
10. Add BEATEN EGGS to large mixing bowl.
11. Measure 2 TEAspoons of OLD BAY and add to large mixing bowl.
12. Measure 1 TEAspoon of WORCESERSHIRE SAUCE and add to large mixing bowl.
13. Measure 1 TEAspoon of TABASCO and add to large mixing bowl.
14. Measure 2 TEAspoons of DIJON MUSTARD and add to large mixing bowl.
15. Peel APPLE and chop into 1/8" x 1/8" PIECES.
16. Add CHOPPED APPLE to large mixing bowl.
17. Dump CRAB MEAT into large mixing bowl.
18. With wooden spoon, lightly mix large mixing bowl INGREDIENTS.
19. Place several paper towels next to large mixing bowl.
20. Reach into large mixing bowl and grab a large handful of MIXTURE.

21. Use your hands to shape MIXTURE into a ½" thick PATTY; it should be smaller around than a hamburger patty and thicker.
22. Pick up 1 PATTY and place it in the middle of the CRUSHED STUFFING in bowl #1.
23. Push down on the PATTY to make sure it gets all covered in STUFFING.
24. With two hands – it could easily fall apart – pick up PATTY and flip it onto its other side. Again, push down on it to ensure coverage.
25. With two hands, pick up PATTY and gently place it on large plate #1.
26. Repeat steps 20-25 to make 6 CRAB CAKES.
27. When all the CRAB CAKES have been completed, wipe off hands with paper towels. Wash hands.
28. Place large frying pan on a stovetop burner.
29. Turn on flame to high heat.
30. Cut 2 TABLEspoons of BUTTER (use the ruler on the wax paper wrapper to measure this) and add to large frying pan.
31. When BUTTER melts, pick up frying pan and tilt so BUTTER coats entire large frying pan.
32. Use thin spatula to place CRAB CAKES in large frying pan.
33. Reduce flame to medium heat.
34. Set oven timer for 3 minutes.
35. Slice each LEMON into 3 wedges for a total of six.
36. When oven timer goes off, use spatula to flip CRAB CAKES.
37. Re-set oven timer for 3 minutes.
38. Rinse off colander. Rinse off large plate.
39. Place LEMON WEDGES on large plate #2.
40. When oven timer goes off, turn off flame.
41. Use thin spatula to move CRAB CAKES to large plate #2.
42. Carry large plate #2 to table.
43. The Appetizer is served!

SALADS

Darren's One-Minute Salad

Darren is a buddy who lives on Shavehead Lake in southwestern Michigan. When he's not selling high-end horse trailers, he's making magic in the kitchen.

Ease: 1 Chef
Cost: $28
Preparation Time: 5 minutes
Cooking Time: Zero

Ingredients:
Mixed Green Salad – 1 Bag pre-washed; 4.29
Grape Tomatoes – 1 Box; $4
Fresh Blue Cheese – 1 Box; $3.95
Chopped Pecans – 1 Bag; $3.99 per 16-ounce bag
Thinly Sliced Purple Onion – ½; $4.29 per bottle
T. Marzetti's French Honey Salad Dressing – 1 bottle; $6.00

Tools, etc:
Large Serving Bowl
Colander (The thingy with all the holes; it's for draining)
Metal Spoon
Cutting Board
Chopping Knife

Directions:
1. Open SALAD BAG and empty SALAD into large serving bowl.
2. Place colander in sink.
3. Pour TOMATOES into colander and wash TOMATOES.
4. If you don't want to cry while chopping PURPLE ONION, take a dinner spoon and suck on it. Seriously.
5. Chop off both ends of the PURPLE ONION. Then, cut the REMAINDER in half.
6. Remove SKIN and throw the skin in the trash.
7. You now have a halved purple onion that has been cut on two sides.
8. Turn ONION so that 1 cut side faces you. Choose 1 UNCUT SIDE.
9. Store half ONION in freezer bag. Store in freezer.
10. Place other half ONION on cutting board.

11. Thinly slice along that uncut side. Think of it like a wet t-shirt contest, only instead of "Skin to Win!" this motto is, "Thin to Win!"
12. Use your fingers to evenly spread out the ONION in the large serving bowl.
13. Furiously scrub hands with DISH SOAP. ONION will stink up your cuticles, which won't go over well later when you try to feed her dessert.
14. Pour TOMATOES into large serving bowl.
15. Add BLUE CHEESE to large serving bowl.
16. Add PECANS to large serving bowl.
17. Toss SALAD.
18. Add SALAD to bowls.
19. Add SALAD DRESSING to salads.
20. Carry salad bowls to table.
21. Salad is served!

Chef Zach's Arugula Salad

Zach McGowan is also an actor, most recently appearing in "Terminator Salvation".
Thanks to this recipe, I learned that I do not hate Arugula. In fact, Arugula is my favorite type of lettuce! (Turns out I hate radicchio.)

Ease: 2 Chefs
Cost: $23
Preparation Time: 20 minutes
Cooking Time: Zero

Ingredients:
Arugula Salad – 1 Bag pre-washed; $4.29
Extra Virgin Olive Oil – 2 TABLEspoons; $6-13 per bottle
Red Onion – 1; $.85
Shredded Parmesan Cheese – 1.5 Cups; $3.99 per 16-ounce bag
White Balsamic Vinegar – 1 TABLEspoon; $4.29 per bottle
Sea Salt – ¼ TEAspoon; $1.34 per shaker

Tools, etc:
Large Serving Bowl
Cutting Board
Chopping Knife
Measuring Spoons
Small Plate – 2
Wooden Spoon

Directions:
1. Open ARUGULA BAG and empty SALAD into large serving bowl.

2. If you don't want to cry while chopping ONIONS, take a dinner spoon and suck on it. Seriously.
3. Chop off both ends of the RED ONION. Then, cut the REMAINDER in half.
4. Remove SKIN and throw the skin in the trash.
5. You now have a halved red onion that has been cut on two sides.
6. Turn ONION so that 1 cut side faces you. Choose 1 UNCUT SIDE.
7. Thinly slice along that uncut side. Place ONION in measuring cup. You want ½ Cup of sliced onions. The point here is to slice the onion as thinly as possible. Think of it like a wet t-shirt contest, only instead of "Skin to Win!" this motto is, "Thin to Win!"
8. Use your fingers to evenly spread out the ONION in the large serving bowl.
9. Furiously scrub hands with DISH SOAP. ONION will stink up your cuticles, which won't go over well later when you try to feed her dessert.
10. Measure 1.5 Cups of PARMESAN CHEESE. Add CHEESE to large serving bowl.
11. Measure 1 TABLEspoon of OLIVE OIL and pour all over SALAD.
12. Measure 1 TABLEspoon of WHITE BALSAMIC VINEGAR and pour over SALAD.
13. Measure ¼ TEAspoon of SEA SALT. Take a pinch and sprinkle it all over the SALAD.
14. Toss SALAD.
15. Add SALAD to bowls.
16. Carry salad bowls to table.
17. Salad is served!

Jamie's Lettuce-less Salad

In case you or Ms. Right Now loathe lettuce.

Ease: 3 Chefs (Lots of chopping)
Cost: $12
Preparation Time: 15 minutes
Cooking Time: Zero

Ingredients:
Tomatoes – 2; $2.99 per pound
Yellow Bell Pepper – 1; $1.50 per pound
Cucumber – 1; .79 each
Carrots – 2; $1.00 each
Thinly Sliced Purple Onion – ½; $1.29 per pound
Salad Dressing of your choice – 1 bottle; $2.00

Tools, etc:
Large Serving Bowl

Colander (The thingy with all the holes; it's for draining)
Paper Towels
Cutting Board
Peeler
Chopping Knife
Metal Spoon

Directions:
1. Open SALAD BAG and empty SALAD into large serving bowl.
2. Place colander in sink.
3. Wash TOMATOES. Pat dry with paper towels.
4. Wash YELLOW PEPPER. Pat dry with paper towel.
5. On the cutting board chop TOMATOES. Throw out TOPS and BOTTOMS of TOMATOES.
6. Run WATER in sink. Rinse off icky, green SEEDS from TOMATOES. Then, drop TOMATOES into colander to dry.
7. Cut open top of YELLOW PEPPER. Pull out and throw out STEM. Shake out SEEDS into trash.
8. On the cutting board, slice YELLOW PEPPER in half. Shake out any remaining SEEDS into trash. Cut out and throw out all WHITE PARTS inside pepper.
9. Chop up YELLOW BELL PEPPER into half-inch wide sections. Next, chop those into half-inch long CHUNKS.
10. Add YELLOW BELL PEPPER to large serving bowl.
11. Use peeler to peel CUCUMBER over the trash pail so the skin gets thrown out in the process.
12. Chop off the top and bottom of the CUCUMBER. Throw them out.
13. Cut CUCUMBER into ¼ inch wide SLICES.
14. Add CUCUMBER to large mixing bowl.
15. Use peeler to peel CARROTS over the trash pail so the skin gets thrown out in the process.
16. Chop off the tops and bottoms of the CARROTS. Throw tops and bottoms out.
17. Cut CARROTS into ¼ inch wide SLICES.
18. Add CARROTS to large mixing bowl.
19. If you don't want to cry while chopping PURPLE ONION, take a dinner spoon and suck on it. Seriously.
20. Chop off both ends of the PURPLE ONION. Then, cut the REMAINDER in half.
21. Remove SKIN and throw the skin in the trash.
22. You now have a halved purple onion that has been cut on two sides.
23. Turn ONION so that 1 cut side faces you. Choose 1 UNCUT SIDE.

24. Store half ONION in freezer bag. Store in freezer.
25. Place other half ONION on cutting board.
26. Thinly slice along that uncut side. The point here is to slice the onion as thinly as possible. Think of it like a wet t-shirt contest, only instead of "Skin to Win!" this motto is, "Thin to Win!"
27. Use your fingers to evenly spread out the ONION in the large serving bowl.
28. Furiously scrub hands with DISH SOAP. ONION will stink up your cuticles, which won't go over well later when you try to feed her dessert.
29. Toss SALAD.
30. Add SALAD to bowls.
31. Add SALAD DRESSING to salads.
32. Carry salad bowls to table.
33. Salad is served!

BEEF

Jerry's Round Steak

Jen Pransky is one of the best coed flag football players I've ever seen. More importantly, she is also a tremendous teammate in the game of life.

Jen more than answered the call when I solicited "a" recipe from each of my female friends. She sent me the 25-page document her mother compiled chronicling her family's cooking history! (Alas, only one other of their recipes – Pransky's Picatta – was sufficiently elementary for Bachelor 101 readers.)

"Thank you," Mary Lou Pransky!

Described as a "great cooking trick for cooks on a budget," this steak recipe is from Jen's late father Jerry. Jen assures me that her Dad "would be thrilled" to be in the book. Having been wowed by the ease and taste of this steak, I'm thrilled to include him.

This is not a "Date Night" meal. The quality of the steak is good, but not great. It's tasty and juicy, but it's no filet or NY Strip. However, it's perfect for a solo weeknight dinner (and possible next day lunch).

Warning: "Top Round" Steak refers to the particular cut of the beef. "Top Round" does not mean "a high quality circle of beef," as I thought. Don't ask how much time I spent in the meat department looking for circular steaks before finally breaking down and asking the supermarket butcher for help.

Ease: 1 Chef
Cost: $33
Preparation Time: 3 minutes
Cooking Time: 20 minutes (2/3 of which are for the baked potatoes)

Ingredients:
Top Round Steak – not more than ½ Inch thick; $6.75
Butter – 8 TABLEspoons "divided"; $5.50 for 4 sticks. ("Divided" means you'll use a total of 8 TABLEspoons, but at different steps in the process)
Sea Salt – No Set Amount; $3.99 per bottle
Cracked Black Pepper – No Set Amount; $3.99 per bottle
Russett Potatoes – 2; $2.00 (a dollar apiece)
Salad – 1 Bag pre-washed; $5
Tomatoes – 2; $2.99 per pound
Salad Dressing – Bottle of your choice; $2

Recommended Wine: Cabernet or, if feeling adventurous, Barbera D' Asti

Tools, etc:
"Astroturf" Sponge (You know, the kind with the green scrubbing side)
Paper Towels

Large Plate
Fork
Large Frying Pan
Small Plate
Measuring Spoons
Cutting Board
Sharp Knife
Colander (the thingy with all the holes; it's for draining things)

Directions:
1. Scrub POTATOES with Astroturf sponge. Pat dry with a paper towel.
2. Place 2 POTATOES on large plate.
3. Take fork and puncture each POTATO in 8 different places.
4. Place large plate in microwave.
5. Cook POTATOES for 14 minutes. (Note: If you were only microwaving 1 POTATO, you'd cook it for 11 minutes. When you microwave additional potatoes, add 3 minutes for each one.)
6. Set oven timer for 12 minutes.
7. Place large frying pan on stovetop burner. Do not turn on flame yet.
8. Unwrap STEAK from plastic.
9. Put colander in sink.
10. Wash TOMATOES. Pat dry with paper towels.
11. Open BAG OF SALAD. Add SALAD to salad bowls.
12. Slice TOMATOES. Throw out TOPS and BOTTOMS of TOMATOES.
13. Run WATER in sink. Rinse off icky, green SEEDS from TOMATOES. Then, drop TOMATOES into colander to dry.
14. When oven timer goes off, turn on flame under frying pan to high heat.
15. Measure 4 TABLEspoons of BUTTER (Use the ruler on the wax paper to do this) and add to frying pan.
16. When BUTTER has melted, use fork to gently lay STEAK into frying pan.
17. Set oven timer for 3 minutes.
18. You do not want to flip the STEAK more than once.
19. When the oven timer goes off, use fork to gently flip STEAK.
20. If you like your STEAK rare, set oven timer for 1 minute.
21. If you like your STEAK medium-rare, set oven timer for 2 minutes.
22. If you like your STEAK medium, set oven timer for 3 minutes.
23. Add TOMATOES to salad bowl.

24. When oven timer goes off, turn off flame.
25. Use fork to move STEAK to dinner plate.
26. Grab the SEA SALT and sprinkle however much you f'ing want over the STEAK. You don't have to worry about what Ms. Right Now likes!
27. Grab the PEPPER and sprinkle away to your breath's content.
28. Use fork to move BAKED POTATO to dinner plate.
29. Add SALAD DRESSING to salad.
30. Carry salad bowl and dinner plate to the couch.
31. Bachelor Dinner is served!

Jamie's Broiled Ribeye Steak

Not every guy has a grill, due to lease restrictions, etc. But everybody has an oven with a broiler, so I decided to go with an easy recipe for the latter.

The broiler is located in the bottom of the oven; that small, seemingly useless door underneath the big one where you cook frozen pizza. Unlike a grill where the flame is below the food, a broiler works with the flame ABOVE the food.

The broiler affords the cook flexibility in terms of heat and proximity to the flame. Most broilers have two temperature settings: HI and LOW. Additionally, the broiler pan can be moved to different slots so as to bring the meat closer to or further from the flame.

Let me start by saying I have always been terrified of the broiler; never used it and wasn't willing to try.

After finally popping my cherry in order to write this book, I am now kicking myself for ignoring the broiler. What a breeze! And the steak tastes great, too.

I combined a dash of fatherly wisdom – thanks, Dad! – with a sprinkle of internet guidance to make this recipe. Simple and yummy, baby.

Ease: 2 Chefs
Cost: $44
Preparation Time: 45 minutes
Cooking Time: 20 minutes, tops. Broiling time for steaks depends on how "done" you want the meat. Rare only needs 7 minutes (3.5 per side) and well done takes 14 minutes. Regardless, the steak needs to cool for 5 minutes after cooking to lock in the juices.

Ingredients:
2 Ribeye Steaks (normally @ 12 oz. Each) – $12.50 per pound
Garlic Salt – 2 tablespoons; $2.99
Butter – 2 tablespoons (hard); $5.50 (for 4 sticks)
Wild Rice – 1 Microwavable Bag; $2.49
Pre-washed Salad – 1 Bag; $5.00
Tomatoes – 2; $2.99 per pound
Salad Dressing – 1 bottle of your choice; $2.00
Take-n-Bake Bread – 1 Loaf; $2.00 (*Found in Bakery section of supermarket*)

Recommended Wine: Cabernet or, if feeling adventurous, Syrah

Tools, etc:
Oven Mitts (2)
Small Plate
Colander
Cutting Board
Knife
Paper Towels
Stopwatch

Directions:

1. 1 hour before you want to eat, place RIBEYES on a plate. Let them sit at room temperature for 45 minutes.
2. Open broiler door and remove the broiler pan. This is what you're going to cook the steak in. Wash broiler pan and dry it with paper towels.
3. Place pan in drying rack next to sink, just to be sure it dries sufficiently.
4. Take a paper towel and check to make sure broiler pan is dry. If not, dry pan.
5. Put on oven mitts. Open broiler door.
6. Grab broiler pan and slide it into the broiler, making sure that the edges of the pan slide into the highest slot. This is important because you want the beef to be as close to the flame as possible.
7. Ask Ms. Right Now how she likes her steak done.
8. Measure ½ tablespoon of GARLIC SALT and sprinkle over one side of RIBEYE.
9. Take PEPPER and crank 5 turns over same side.
10. Rub GARLIC SALT and PEPPER into the meat with your fingertips.
11. Place 1 tablespoon of BUTTER on small plate. Put in microwave. Heat for 20 seconds.
12. Remove butter from microwave. Most should be melted into liquid.
13. Carefully drip half the BUTTER onto one RIBEYE. Take any SOLID BUTTER left on plate, and rub it into non-buttered portions of RIBEYE.
14. Flip RIBEYE over onto the other side. Repeat step 14.
15. Start on other RIBEYE and repeat steps 12 – 15.
16. Grab broiler pan. Place RIBEYES in pan.
17. Stop and consider how you want the STEAKS cooked. You will need 7-minutes for RARE, 10 minutes for MEDIUM and 14 minutes for WELL DONE. The STEAKS will need 5 minutes to cool off when they come out of the oven. So, do the math and figure out when to start broiling your steaks.
18. 10 minutes before you want to start broiling, pre-heat broiler to 350 degrees.
19. At same time, pre-heat oven to 350 degrees. This is for the bread.

20. Put colander in sink.
21. Open BAG OF SALAD. Add SALAD to salad bowls.
22. On the cutting board chop TOMATOES. Throw out TOPS and BOTTOMS of TOMATOES.
23. Run WATER in sink. Rinse off icky, green SEEDS from TOMATOES. Then, drop TOMATOES into colander to dry.
24. When you are ready to start the STEAKS, put on oven mitts.
25. Open broiler door. Slide the broiler pan out.
26. With one hand grab plate with the RIBEYES and with the other hand grab fork.
27. Carefully place each RIBEYE onto the pan. This will cause hissing and popping. If any buttery goop sticks to the plate the steaks were on, scrape up the goop with a knife and smear it onto any bare parts of the steak.
28. Slide the pan back in. Close the broiler door.
29. Set oven timer. For RARE, you need to flip them at the 3.5-minute mark. For MEDIUM RARE, you need to flip them at the 5-minute mark. For WELL DONE, you need to flip them at the 7-minute mark.
30. Open TAKE-N-BAKE BREAD.
31. Open oven door. Slide out rack.
32. Place BREAD on rack. Slide in rack. Close oven door. Take off oven mitts.
33. Start stopwatch. BREAD needs to be cooked for 15 minutes.
34. When oven timer goes off, put on oven mitts and grab a fork.
35. Open the broiler door. Slide out pan.
36. Use the fork to flip the STEAKS. Then, slide in pan. Close door.
37. Reset the oven timer for the same amount of time as before.
38. Add TOMATOES to salad bowls.
39. When oven timer goes off, turn off broiler.
40. Put on oven mitts and grab a fork.
41. Open the broiler door, slide out pan and, with the fork, pick up each steak and put them on a clean plate.
42. Let the steaks and potatoes cool for 5 minutes. Set oven timer.
43. When stopwatch reaches 15 minutes, turn off oven.
44. Put on oven mitt. Open oven door. Slide out rack.
45. Remove BREAD and place on cutting board.
46. Slide in rack. Close oven door. Take off oven mitts.
47. Slice ¼ Loaf of BREAD. Put 2 SLICES on each dinner plate.

48. Rip top of BAG OF RICE according to directions. Cook in microwave for 90 seconds.
49. Add SALAD DRESSING to salads.
50. When RICE is done, remove bag and tear off top. Be careful, this mofo is hot!
51. Pour half the RICE onto each dinner plate.
52. Carry SALADS out to table.
53. When oven timer goes off, place a RIBEYE on each dinner plate.
54. Carry out dinner plates.
55. Dinner is served!

Jamie's Spicy Meatloaf

Don't laugh! Meatloaf is one of the all-time great comfort foods. On a cold, dark day when she's feeling down, you can come to the rescue with an oldie but goodie. After dinner she'll be looking to provide you with some, uh, comfort.

Besides, you can freeze half the meatloaf <u>before</u> you cook it, providing you with at least two big meals down the road.

You do not <u>have</u> to have a loaf baking tin to make this, but the tin makes the job a little easier by shaping the meat. If you just want to use a large baking dish (which is what I did the first time), simply squish the meat into the shape of a small loaf of bread.

Ease: 4 Chefs (Only because there's a ton of veggie chopping. That downer is rectified, though, by the unabashed fun of squishing up hamburger meat and mashing it with the other ingredients.)
Cost: $64
Preparation Time: 45 minutes
Cooking Time: 70 minutes, total, including the potatoes. The meatloaf needs to sit for 10 minutes after cooking to lock in the juices.

Ingredients:
Ground Beef – 1.5 pounds; $7 (Sells for $3.50 per pound)
Spicy Italian Sausage – 3 links (ripped out of casing); $3.29 per package of 5
Egg – 1 (slightly beaten); $3.49 per dozen
Yellow Bell Pepper – 1; $1.50 per pound
Celery – 1 stalk; $1.49 for @ 8 stalks
Carrot – 1; 89 cents per pound
Yellow Onion – 2 (it may look more brown than yellow); $1.29 per pound
Cayenne Pepper – 1 TABLEspoon; $6.29 per bottle
Rosemary – 1 TABLEspoon; $2.49 per bottle
Sage – 1 TABLEspoon; $2.49 per bottle
Bread Crumbs – ½ Cup; $1.79 per box
Minced Garlic – 3 TEAspoons; $1.99-6.99 per jar
Ketchup – ¼ Cup; $3.00
Croutons – 2 Cups; $1.50 per box (These are found in the vegetable section of

the supermarket, near the fresh basil, rosemary, etc. You can go with plain or pick from several different flavors of croutons.)
Russet (Baked) Potatoes – 4; $4.00 ($1 each)
Pre-washed Salad – 1 Bag; $5.00
Tomatoes – 2; $2.99 per pound
Salad Dressing – 1 bottle of your choice; $2.00
Take-n-Bake Bread – 1 Loaf; $2.00 (*Found in Bakery section of supermarket*)
Butter – 4 TABLEspoons; $5.50 per package of four sticks

Recommended Wine: Zinfandel or, if feeling adventurous, Shiraz (Shiraz is Australian Syrah, by the way.)

Tools, etc:
Small Bowl
Paper Towels
Cutting Board
Colander
Paring Knife
Large Mixing Bowl
Loaf Baking Pan
Tin Foil
Oven Mitts (2)
Peeler
Wooden Spoon
Sponge with "Astroturf"
Large Plate
Fork
Small Plate

Directions:

1. Crack EGG into small bowl. Use fork to beat EGG.

2. Wash BELL PEPPER and CELERY. Pat dry with paper towels.

3. Cut open top of BELL PEPPER. Pull out and throw out STEM. Shake out SEEDS into trash.

4. Slice BELL PEPPER in half. Shake out remaining SEEDS into trash. Cut out and throw out all WHITE PARTS inside pepper.

5. Chop up BELL PEPPER into half-inch wide sections. Next, chop those into 1/8" x 1/8" strips, about the size of the onions on a McDonald's hamburger.

6. Add BELL PEPPER to large mixing bowl.

7. Chop up 1 stalk of CELERY into half-inch wide sections, then chop those into 1/8" x 1/8" strips.

8. Add CELERY to large mixing bowl.

9. Add 1.5 pounds of GROUND BEEF to large mixing bowl.

10. Take knife and slice open the SKIN on 3 links of SPICY SAUSAGE.

11. Squeeze out the SAUSAGE MEAT into large mixing bowl.
12. Add 1 TABLEspoon of CAYENNE PEPPER to large mixing bowl.
13. Add 1 TABLEspoon of ROSEMARY to large mixing bowl.
14. Add 1 TABLEspoon of SAGE to large mixing bowl.
15. Add ½ Cup of BREAD CRUMBS to large mixing bowl.
16. Add 3 TEAspoons of MINCED GARLIC to large mixing bowl.
17. Take peeler and peel 1 CARROT.
18. Slice CARROT in half lengthwise. Chop CARROT HALVES into 1/8" x 1/8" chunks.
19. Pre-heat oven to 350 degrees.
20. This is totally serious: Put a metal spoon in your mouth. This will help keep you from crying while chopping onions.
21. Chop off both ends of ONION. Peel the SKIN off the ONION. Peel 1 layer off the ONION.
22. Slice ONION in half. Look for a thin TUBE of onion in the center. Throw that piece in trash.
23. Chop ONION into 1/8" x 1/8" PIECES.
24. Add CHOPPED ONION to large mixing bowl.
25. Repeat steps 25 – 28 with the second ONION.
26. Add EGG to large mixing bowl.
27. Using wooden spoon, thoroughly mix all ingredients in large mixing bowl.
28. Position loaf baking tin on counter near large mixing bowl.
29. Add 2 Cups of CROUTONS to the loaf baking tin.
30. Use your fingers to line the bottom with the CROUTONS, just like tiles on a floor.
31. Wash your HANDS.
32. Now for the fun part! Stick your HANDS into the MIXTURE and start squishing! You have to make sure everything is mixed into one big blob.
33. Pick up the BLOB and stuff it into the loaf baking tin.
34. Use your hands to level MEATLOAF and make sure MEATLOAF is the same height throughout the loaf baking tin.
35. **STOP!** If you want to freeze half the MEATLOAF, this is the time to do so. Place tin foil on the counter. Cut the MEATLOAF in half, remove half and wrap it in tin foil. Place it in the freezer.

    Now, back to everybody's instructions.
36. Wash your HANDS! And then wash off the faucet knob (and freezer door handle, if you froze half) because it is covered in goop.
37. Put on oven mitt. Open oven door. Slide out top rack.

38. Place baking tin on top rack. Slide in rack. Close oven door. Take off oven mitt.
39. Set oven timer for 50 minutes.
40. Scrub POTATOES with Astroturf sponge. Pat dry with a paper towel.
41. Place 4 POTATOES on large plate.
42. Take fork and puncture each POTATO in 8 different places.
43. Place large plate in microwave.
44. Place colander in sink.
45. On cutting board, slice TOMATOES. Throw out both the tops and bottoms of TOMATOES.
46. Turn on WATER in sink. Take SLICED TOMATOES in your fingers and rinse off the icky, green SEEDS.
47. Drop clean TOMATOES into colander to dry.
48. Open SALAD BAG. Add SALAD to two salad bowls.
49. When oven timer goes off, open TAKE-N-BAKE BREAD.
50. Put on oven mitt. Open oven door. Slide out bottom rack.
51. Place BREAD on bottom rack. Slide in rack. Close oven door. Take off oven mitt.
52. Re-set oven timer for 10 minutes.
53. Microwave POTATOES for 20 minutes. (Note: If you were only making 1 POTATO, you'd cook it for 11 minutes. When you microwave additional potatoes, add 3 minutes for each one.)
54. Cut 4 TABLEspoons of BUTTER (Use the ruler on the wax paper wrapper to measure this) and put BUTTER on small plate for later.
55. When oven timer goes off, put on oven mitts.
56. Open oven door. Slide out rack. Remove baking tin and place on stovetop burners. Close oven door.
57. Re-set oven timer for 5 minutes. Turn up oven's heat to 500 degrees. This is to finish cooking the BREAD.
58. When the oven timer goes off, turn off oven.
59. Put on oven mitt. Open oven door.
60. Slide out bottom rack.
61. Remove BREAD and place on cutting board.
62. Close oven door. Take off oven mitt.
63. Add TOMATOES to salad bowls.
64. Slice ¼ Loaf of BREAD. Put 2 SLICES on each dinner plate.
65. When microwave stops, place 1 POTATO on each dinner plate.

66. Slice open a 2 inch seam in top of each potato to let them cool.
67. Add SALAD DRESSING to SALADS.
68. Carry SALADS and butter plate out to table.
69. Cut and place 2 slices of MEATLOAF on each dinner plate.
70. Carry out dinner plates.
71. Dinner is served!

POULTRY

Barton's Russian Chicken

As a tennis star at Notre Dame, Tracy Barton liked to dispatch her opponents quickly without breaking a sweat. Now an All-American mother of three girls, Tracy likes to cook her meals the same way.

This dish will make Ms. Right Now think you worked <u>a lot</u> harder than you did.

Ease: 1 Chef
Cost: $50
Preparation Time: 5 minutes
Cooking Time: 60 minutes

Ingredients:
Skinless/Boneless Chicken Breasts – 4; $12.99 for package of 8
Russian Salad Dressing – 1 bottle; $1.99. *This stuff is really hard to find in the Salad Dressing Aisle, which is silly considering the Cold War is long over. Now, Iraqi Salad Dressing, I could understand being difficult to locate…*
Apricot Preserves – 1 jar; $2.36
Lipton Onion Soup Mix – 1 packet; $1.99 per box of two packets
Mrs. Dash Seasoning – 1 TEAspoon; $3.99 per bottle
Butter – 1 tablespoon; $5.50 (for 4 sticks)
Rice Pilaf – 1 Microwavable Bag; $2.49
Pre-washed Salad – 1 bag; $5
Tomatoes – 4; $2.99
Salad Dressing – 1 bottle of your choice; $2.00 (Probably don't wanna serve Russian Dressing…)
Non-Stick Spray – 1 can; $4.99
Take-n-Bake Bread – 1 Loaf; $2 (*Found in Bakery section of supermarket*)

Recommended Wine: Zinfandel or, if feeling adventurous, Syrah

Tools, etc:
Mixing Bowl
Large Baking Dish
Paring Knife
Tin Foil
Stopwatch
Colander (Plastic thingy with the holes in it)
Oven Mitt – 2
Wooden Spoon
Cutting Board

Instant-Read Meat Thermometer

Directions:

1. Pre-heat oven to 325.
2. Wash off CHICKEN BREASTS in sink. Pat dry with paper towels.
3. Spray large baking dish with NON-STICK SPRAY.
4. Add CHICKEN to baking dish.
5. Pour Bottle of RUSSIAN DRESSING into mixing bowl.
6. Pour Jar of APRICOT PRESERVES into mixing bowl.
7. Pour 1 Packet of FRENCH ONION SOUP MIX into mixing bowl.
8. Mix INGREDIENTS thoroughly. SAUCE will turn a deep red color. This is some seriously sticky shit, so make sure to clean up spills right away.
9. Pour SAUCE all over CHICKEN. Ensure that every bit of chicken is covered in the goop; this is the key to making a tender bird.
10. Cover baking dish with tin foil.
11. Put on oven mitt. Open oven door and slide out rack. Place baking dish on rack. Slide in rack. Close door.
12. Set oven timer for 30 minutes.
13. Put cutting board on counter.
14. When oven timer goes off, put on oven mitts.
15. Open oven door and slide out rack. Take baking dish and place it on cool burners. Slide in rack. Close door.
16. Remove tin foil. Throw out tin foil.
17. Open oven door. Slide out top rack. Place baking dish on rack. Slide in rack.
18. Close door. Take off oven mitts.
19. Set oven timer for 20 minutes.
20. Open BAG OF SALAD. Add to two salad bowls.
21. Wash TOMATOES. Dry TOMATOES with paper towel. Place on cutting board.
22. Place colander in sink.
23. On cutting board, slice TOMATOES. Throw out both the tops and bottoms of TOMATOES.
24. Turn on WATER in sink. Take SLICED TOMATOES in your fingers and rinse off the icky, green SEEDS. Then, drop clean TOMATOES into colander to dry.
25. Fill frying pan with 4 Cups of WATER. Place frying pan on burner. Don't turn on flame yet.
26. When oven timer goes off, open TAKE-N-BAKE BREAD.
27. Put on oven mitts. Open oven door and slide out bottom rack.

28. Place BREAD on bottom rack. Slide in bottom rack. Close oven door. Take off oven mitts.
29. Re-set oven timer for 10 minutes.
30. Add equal amounts of CHOPPED TOMATOES to salad bowls.
31. When oven timer goes off, put on oven mitts.
32. Open oven door and slide out top rack. Place baking dish onto stovetop burners. Slide in rack. Close door.
33. Stick instant-read meat thermometer into a CHICKEN BREAST. The temperature must be 160 degrees or Ms. Right Now may die.
34. If the temperature is 160 or higher, the chicken is done. But if the temperature is lower than 160, return the baking dish back to the oven for 5 minutes.
35. Once the CHICKEN is done, re-set oven timer for 5 minutes. Turn up oven's heat to 500 degrees. This is to finish cooking the BREAD.
36. When timer goes off, turn off oven.
37. Put on oven mitt. Open oven door. Slide out bottom rack.
38. Remove BREAD and place on cutting board.
39. Slide in rack. Close oven door. Take off oven mitt.
40. Add SALAD DRESSING to SALAD.
41. Carry salad bowls and butter plate to table.
42. When oven timer goes off, grab BAG of MICROWAVABLE RICE.
43. Open top sides as instructed. Put BAG in microwave and cook for 90 seconds.
44. Slice ¼ Loaf of BREAD. Put 2 SLICES on each dinner plate.
45. When RICE is done, remove bag and tear off top. Be careful, this mofo is hot! Let cool.
46. Place 1 CHICKEN BREAST on each dinner plate.
47. Pour ½ bag of RICE onto each dinner plate.
48. Carry dinner plates to table.
49. Dinner is served!

Curt's Crumby Chicken

After U.S. Army Major Curt Croom (Retired) arrived in Japan in 1993 to be my boss, he did his best to show his 23-year old underling how to be a man. He spoke reverentially about cars, guns, huntin' and fishin', but quickly realized if not for my love of sports and women I might be gay.

Unbowed, Curt tried to teach me skills and habits other men would find impressive. He showed me how to fix stuff, urged me to take golf lessons, encouraged me to smoke cigars and begged me to start drinking bourbon.

Fifteen years later, I can change a light bulb solo, occasionally crack 100 in golf, and still turn green from a stogie. But I do drink bourbon! But the latter had nothing to do with Curt and everything to do with my jackass friends in LA who refused to buy my requested beer when it was their round.

Curt also told me that panties would come flying off if I learned to cook. Why, oh, why didn't I listen to this man more often???

This recipe is my favorite in Bachelor 101.

Ease: 1 Chef
Cost: $45
Preparation Time: 10 minutes
Cooking Time: 60 minutes

Ingredients:
Boneless, Skinless Chicken Breasts – 4; $12.99 for eight
Ritz Crackers – 1 Sleeve; $3.49 per box
Butter – 8 TABLEspoons "divided"; $5.50 per package of 4 sticks ("Divided" means the ingredients will be used at different steps in the process)
Black Pepper – 2 TABLEspoons; $1.29 per bottle
Garlic Salt – 1 TABLEspoon; $3.00 per bottle
Wild Rice – 1 Microwavable Bag; $2.49
Pre-washed Salad – 1 Bag; $5
Tomatoes – 2; $2.99 per pound
Salad Dressing – Bottle of your choice; $2
Take-n-Bake Bread – 1 Loaf; $2.00 (*Found in Bakery section of supermarket*)
Non-Stick Spray; $4.99

Wine Recommendation: Merlot or, if feeling adventurous, Syrah

Tools, etc:
Large Plate – 2
Large Baking Dish
Paper Towels
Small Plate - 2
Measuring Spoons
Ziploc Bag
Basting Brush
Fork
Colander (the thingy with all the holes; it's for draining stuff)
Cutting Board
Paring Knife
Instant-Read Meat Thermometer

Directions:
1. Pre-heat oven to 350 degrees.
2. Spray large baking pan with NON-STICK SPRAY.

3. Wash CHICKEN BREASTS under cold water in sink. Dry BREASTS with paper towels and place BREASTS on large plate #1.
4. Wash HANDS. Then, wash faucet knob afterwards because it'll be GROSS from your fingers getting slimy after handling the chicken.
5. Open one sleeve of RITZ CRACKERS and pour into Ziploc bag.
6. Seal Ziploc bag. Crush CRACKERS in Ziploc bag.
7. Cut 4 TABLEspoons of BUTTER (Use the ruler on the wax paper wrapper to measure this) and put BUTTER on small plate #1.
8. Place small plate in microwave and cook for 30 seconds.
9. Measure 2 TABLEspoons of BLACK PEPPER and add to Ziploc bag.
10. Measure 1 TABLEspoon of GARLIC SALT and add to Ziploc bag.
11. Pour Ziploc bag CONTENTS onto large plate #2.
12. Use basting brush to coat both sides of a BREAST with BUTTER.
13. With a fork, pick up BREAST and place it in the middle of the CRUSHED CRACKERS on large plate #2.
14. Push down on the BREAST to make sure it gets all crackery.
15. With a fork, flip BREAST onto its other side. Again, push down on it.
16. Use fork to move BREAST (it should be practically covered on both sides with CRUSHED CRACKERS) to large baking dish.
17. Repeat steps 12 – 16 with the remaining 3 BREASTS.
18. Wash hands, as they're probably a little greasy.
19. Put on oven mitt. Open oven door. Slide out rack.
20. Place large baking dish on rack. Slide in rack. Close oven door.
21. Set oven timer for 50 minutes. Take off oven mitt.
22. Wash TOMATOES. Pat dry with paper towels.
23. Slice 4 TABLEspoons of BUTTER and place on small plate #2 for later.
24. Put colander in sink.
25. Open BAG OF SALAD. Add SALAD to salad bowls.
26. On the cutting board chop TOMATOES. Throw out TOPS and BOTTOMS of TOMATOES.
27. Run WATER in sink. Rinse off icky, green SEEDS from TOMATOES. Then, drop TOMATOES into colander to dry.
28. Rinse off cutting board.
29. When oven timer goes off, open TAKE-N-BAKE BREAD.
30. Put on oven mitt. Open oven door. Slide out bottom rack.

31. Place BREAD on bottom rack. Slide in rack. Close oven door.
32. Re-set oven timer for 10 minutes. Take off oven mitt.
33. Add TOMATOES to salad bowls.
34. When oven timer goes off, put on oven mitt. Open oven door. Slide out rack with large baking dish.
35. Place large baking dish on stovetop burners so the BREASTS will cool.
36. Slide in rack. Close oven door.
37. Stick instant-read meat thermometer into a CHICKEN BREAST. The temperature must be 160 degrees or Ms. Right Now might die.
38. If the temperature is 160 or higher, the chicken is done. But if the temperature is lower than 160, return the baking dish back to the oven for 5 minutes.
39. Once the CHICKEN is done, re-set oven timer for 5 minutes. Turn up oven's heat to 500 degrees. This is to finish cooking the BREAD.
40. Add SALAD DRESSING to SALADS.
41. Rip top of BAG OF RICE according to directions. Cook in microwave for 90 seconds.
42. Carry butter plate and salad bowls to table.
43. When RICE is done, remove bag and tear off top. Be careful, this mofo is hot!
44. Pour half the RICE onto each dinner plate.
45. With the thin spatula (this lets you keep more of the crackery stuff that's on the bottom side) place 1 BREAST on each dinner plate.
46. When timer goes off, turn off oven.
47. Put on oven mitt. Open oven door. Slide out bottom rack.
48. Remove BREAD and place on cutting board.
49. Slide in rack. Close oven door. Take off oven mitt.
50. Slice ¼ Loaf of BREAD. Put 2 SLICES on each dinner plate.
51. Carry dinner plates to table.
52. Dinner is served!

Susan's World's Greatest Chicken

Susan Guibert, Super Mom/Super Publicist, made up this recipe in ten seconds when her daughter – heading for the school bus – reminded Susan she needed a recipe for a class cookbook that day.
    Maybe I should add "Super Genius" to her description!

Ease: 1 Chef
Cost: $44
Preparation Time: 10 minutes
Cooking Time: 60 minutes

Ingredients:
Boneless, Skinless Chicken Breasts – 4; $12.99 for eight
Ranch Dressing – 1/3 Cup; $2.00 per bottle
Italian Bread Crumbs – 1 Cup; $2.99
Wild Rice – 1 Microwavable Bag; $2.49
Pre-washed Salad – 1 Bag; $5
Tomatoes – 2; $2.99 per pound
Salad Dressing – Bottle of your choice (probably don't want Ranch!); $2
Take-n-Bake Bread – 1 Loaf; $2.00 (*Found in Bakery section of supermarket*)
Butter – 4 TABLEspoons; $5.50 per package of 4 sticks
Non-Stick Spray; $4.99

Wine Recommendation: Cabernet or, if feeling adventurous, Syrah

Tools, etc:
Large Plate – 2
Large Baking Dish
Paper Towels
Small Plate - 2
Measuring Cup
Basting Brush
Fork
Colander (the thingy with all the holes; it's for draining stuff)
Cutting Board
Paring Knife
Instant-Read Meat Thermometer

Directions:
1. Pre-heat oven to 350 degrees.
2. Spray large baking pan with NON-STICK SPRAY.
3. Wash CHICKEN BREASTS under cold water in sink. Dry BREASTS with paper towels and place BREASTS on large plate #1.
4. Wash HANDS. Then, wash faucet knob afterwards because it'll be GROSS from your fingers getting slimy after handling the chicken.
5. Measure 1 Cup of BREAD CRUMBS and add to large plate #2.
6. Measure 1/3 Cup of RANCH DRESSING.
7. Use basting brush to coat both sides of a BREAST with RANCH.
8. With a fork, pick up BREAST and place it in the middle of the BREAD CRUMBS on large plate 2.
9. Push down on the BREAST to make sure it gets all CRUMBY.
10. With a fork, flip BREAST onto its other side. Again, push down on it.
11. Use fork to move BREAST (it should be practically covered on both sides with BREAD CRUMBS) to large baking dish.

12. Repeat steps 7 – 11 with the remaining 3 BREASTS.
13. Wash hands, as they're probably a little sticky.
14. Put on oven mitt. Open oven door. Slide out rack.
15. Place large baking dish on rack. Slide in rack. Close oven door.
16. Set oven timer for 50 minutes. Take off oven mitt.
17. Rinse out measuring cup.
18. Wash TOMATOES. Pat dry with paper towels.
19. Slice 4 TABLEspoons of BUTTER and place on small plate #2 for later.
20. Put colander in sink.
21. Open BAG OF SALAD. Add SALAD to salad bowls.
22. On the cutting board chop TOMATOES. Throw out TOPS and BOTTOMS of TOMATOES.
23. Run WATER in sink. Rinse off icky, green SEEDS from TOMATOES. Then, drop TOMATOES into colander to dry.
24. Rinse off cutting board.
25. When oven timer goes off, open TAKE-N-BAKE BREAD.
26. Put on oven mitt. Open oven door. Slide out bottom rack.
27. Place BREAD on bottom rack. Slide in rack. Close oven door.
28. Re-set oven timer for 10 minutes. Take off oven mitt.
29. Add TOMATOES to salad bowls.
30. When oven timer goes off, put on oven mitt. Open oven door. Slide out rack with large baking dish.
31. Place large baking dish on stovetop burners.
32. Slide in rack. Close oven door.
33. Stick instant-read meat thermometer into a BREAST. The temperature must be 160 degrees or Ms. Right Now might die.
34. If the temperature is 160 or higher, the chicken is done. But if the temperature is lower than 160, return the baking dish back to the oven for 5 minutes.
35. Once the CHICKEN is done, re-set oven timer for 5 minutes. Turn up oven's heat to 500 degrees. This is to finish cooking the BREAD.
36. Add SALAD DRESSING to SALADS.
37. Rip top of BAG OF RICE according to directions. Cook in microwave for 90 seconds.
38. Carry butter plate and salad bowls to table.
39. When RICE is done, remove bag and tear off top. Be careful, this mofo is hot!
40. Pour half the RICE onto each dinner plate.

41. With the thin spatula (this lets you keep more of the CRUMBY STUFF that's on the bottom side) place 1 BREAST on each dinner plate.
42. When timer goes off, turn off oven.
43. Put on oven mitt. Open oven door. Slide out bottom rack.
44. Remove BREAD and place on cutting board.
45. Slide in rack. Close oven door. Take off oven mitt.
46. Slice ¼ Loaf of BREAD. Put 2 SLICES on each dinner plate.
47. Carry dinner plates to table.
48. Dinner is served!

Monica's Chicken Parm

I sprained my ankle during a wrestling practice in my junior year at Notre Dame. A gorgeous angel, er, athletic trainer, Monica (Earley) Macy attended to the injury. My ankle healed fine, but I still asked to get taped every day throughout senior year…as long as Monica was the trainer on duty! Now, she's helping heal the injuries I inflict on my kitchen.

I've made this meal more often than any other in *Bachelor 101*. It's so damn easy.

Ease: 1 Chef
Cost: $53
Preparation Time: 10 minutes
Cooking Time: 45 minutes (Most of which is boiling water for pasta)

Ingredients:
Pre-cooked Breaded Chicken Breast Filets – 1 bag; $7.99 (Not the perfectly circular chicken patties you ate in the dining hall at college.) *You will find these in the frozen food section in the glass cases.*
Spaghetti – 1 box (16 oz.); $2.55 (If you want tons of leftovers, make all the Spaghetti; if not, just use half the box)
Spaghetti Sauce – 8 TABLE spoons; $3.19 per jar
Red Pesto sauce – 4 TABLEspoons; $4.99. *This is found in the refrigerated Italian Section near fresh pasta, etc.*
Shredded Parmesan Cheese – $3.99 per 6-ounce bag (not the Green Can that's been in your parents' fridge your whole life; get the fresh stuff)
Provolone Cheese – 4 Slices; $1.75 per ¼ pound of sliced cheese from Deli
Salad – 1 bag pre-washed; $5
Salad Dressing – Your choice; $2
Tomatoes – 2; $2.99 per pound
Butter – 1 stick; $5.50 (for 4 sticks)
Sea Salt; $4.99
No-stick Spray – 1 Can; $4.99
Take-n-Bake Bread – 1 Loaf; $2 (*Found in Bakery section of supermarket*)

Wine Recommendation: Zinfandel or, if feeling adventurous, Malbec

Tools, etc:
Large Pasta Pot
Oven Mitt – 2
Large Baking Dish
Colander (the thingy with all the holes; it's for draining stuff)
Paper Towels
Small Plate
Cutting Board
Paring Knife
Measuring Spoon
Stopwatch
Tongs
Spatula
Instant-Read Meat Thermometer

Directions:

1. Fill the large pasta pot with as much WATER as the pasta directions say.
2. Place large pasta pot on a burner. Cover pot. Crank flame to high heat. It should take 20-25 minutes for WATER to boil.
3. Check CHICKEN BAG for cooking directions. Pre-heat oven to whatever temperature is listed in the instructions.
4. Spray large baking pan with NON-STICK SPRAY.
5. Place 4 CHICKEN BREASTS in the large baking dish.
6. Scoop 1 TABLEspoon of RED PESTO and spread it all over a BREAST.
7. Repeat step 6 for the other BREASTS.
8. Scoop 2 TABLEspoons of SPAGHETTI SAUCE and spread it all over a BREAST.
9. Repeat step 8 for the other BREASTS.
10. Put on oven mitts. Open oven door. Slide out top rack.
11. Place baking dish on top rack.
12. Slide in rack. Close oven door. Take off oven mitts.
13. Set oven timer for 3 minutes LESS than whatever time is listed in instructions on CHICKEN BAG.
14. Place colander in sink.
15. Wash TOMATOES. Pat dry with paper towels.
16. Cut 7 TABLEspoons of BUTTER (Use the ruler on the wax paper wrapper to measure this) and put BUTTER on small plate for later.
17. Open BAG OF SALAD. Add SALAD to salad bowls.

18. On the cutting board chop TOMATOES. Throw out TOPS and BOTTOMS of TOMATOES.
19. Run WATER in sink. Rinse off icky, green SEEDS from TOMATOES. Then, drop TOMATOES into colander to dry.
20. Rinse off cutting board.
21. When WATER boils, uncover pot and add 2 TABLEspoons of SEA SALT.
22. Add half or whole BOX of SPAGHETTI.
23. Set stopwatch for time given in spaghetti instructions. Stir SPAGAHETTI occasionally to keep noodles from sticking.
24. Open TAKE-N-BAKE BREAD.
25. Put on oven mitts. Open oven door. Slide out bottom rack.
26. Place BREAD on bottom rack. Slide in rack. Close oven door. Take off oven mitts.
27. Open PARMESAN CHEESE.
28. When oven timer goes off, put on oven mitts. Open oven door and slide out top rack.
29. Move large baking dish onto cool stovetop burners.
30. Slide in top rack. Close oven door. Take off oven mitts.
31. Stick instant-read meat thermometer into a BREAST. The temperature must be 160 degrees or Ms. Right Now might die.
32. If the temperature is 160 or higher, the chicken is done. But if the temperature is lower than 160, return the baking dish back to the oven for 5 minutes.
33. Once the CHICKEN is done, smother BREASTS with PARMESAN. Seriously, use as much as you want.
34. Place 1 slice of PROVOLONE on each BREAST.
35. Put on oven mitts. Open oven door. Slide out top rack.
36. Place large baking dish on top rack. Slide in rack. Close oven door.
37. Re-set oven timer for 3 minutes. Take off oven mitts.
38. Add CHOPPED TOMATOES to salad bowls.
39. Rinse out colander. Leave colander in sink.
40. When oven timer goes off, put on oven mitts. Open oven door. Slide out top rack.
41. Place large baking dish on stovetop burners so the BREASTS will cool.
42. Slide in rack. Close oven door. Take off oven mitts.
43. Re-set oven timer for 5 minutes. Turn up oven's heat to 500 degrees. This is to finish cooking the BREAD.
44. Add SALAD DRESSING to SALADS.
45. When stopwatch goes off, turn off flame under pasta pot.

46. Put on oven mitts.
47. Uncover pasta pot and carry pasta pot to sink.
48. Pour WATER and PASTA into colander.
49. Shake colander 3 times. Take off oven mitts.
50. Add 3 TABLEspoons of BUTTER to SPAGHETTI. Use fork to stir in till butter melts.
51. Carry butter plate and salad bowls to table.
52. When oven timer goes off, turn off oven.
53. Put on oven mitt. Open oven door. Slide out bottom rack.
54. Remove BREAD and place on cutting board.
55. Slide in rack. Close oven door. Take off oven mitt.
56. Slice ¼ Loaf of BREAD. Put 2 SLICES on each dinner plate.
57. Use the tongs to move half the SPAGHETTI onto each dinner plate.
58. With the spatula, place 1 BREAST on each dinner plate.
59. Carry dinner plates to table.
60. Dinner is served!

Emily's "Seal The Deal" Chicken

Emily (Swenke) Biggins is a cute real estate agent who cooks up a storm. Maybe her husband Byron should write a book for the rest of us. By the way, Emily named this recipe. Game on!
This meal looks scary. It isn't. So easy. Ms. Right Now will be blown away.

Ease: 1 Chef
Cost: $50
Preparation Time: 20 minutes
Cooking Time: 20 minutes per pound, so @ 60-80 minutes

Ingredients:
One Whole Chicken – (3-4 pounds); $ 12.75
Butter – 7 TABLEspoons "divided"; $5.50 for 4 sticks. ("Divided" means
The ingredients will be used at different steps in the process)
Sea Salt – ½ TEAspoon; $3.99 per bottle
Fresh Rosemary – 2 TABLEspoons; $1.99 per package. *This is found in the Produce section, near the pre-washed salads.*
Fresh Sage – 2 TABLEspoons; $1.99 per package
Fresh Thyme – 2 TABLEspoons; $1.99 per package
Yellow Rice – 1 Microwavable Bag; $2.49
Pre-washed Salad – 1 Bag; $5
Tomatoes – 2; $2.99 per pound
Salad Dressing – Bottle of your choice; $2

Pam (non-stick spray); $4.99
Take-n-Bake Bread – 1 loaf; $2 (*Available in Bakery section of supermarket*)

Recommended Wine: Cabernet or, if feeling adventurous, Dolcetto

Tools, etc:
Paper Towels
Large Baking Dish
Small Plate – 2
Basting Brush
Measuring Spoons
Oven Mitt – 2
Cutting Board
Sharp Knife
Colander (the thingy with all the holes; it's for draining things)
Baster
Instant-Read Meat Thermometer

Directions:

1. Above the sink, reach inside CHICKEN and remove the INNARDS. (You will not do anything more disgusting than this in this book, I swear to you.) Throw out INNARDS.

2. Wash CHICKEN. This means, run the WATER and be sure to thoroughly rinse every single bit of CHICKEN, including the CAVITY from which you just removed the innards.

3. Dry CHICKEN with paper towels.

4. Pre-heat oven to 375 degrees.

5. Spray large baking dish with the NON-STICK SPRAY.

6. Place CHICKEN in large baking dish so that the BREAST is up (Hint: the bony ends of the LEGS should point toward you). Be sure to tuck the LEGS inside the baking dish.

7. Slice 2 TABLEspoons of BUTTER (Use the ruler on the wax paper wrapper to do this) and add the BUTTER to small plate #1.

8. Cook BUTTER in microwave for 30 seconds to melt it.

9. Use basting brush to cover outside of CHICKEN with MELTED BUTTER. As Homer would say, "Hmmm, butter." When it looks like the whole thing is covered, you will still have some butter on the plate. Just hold the plate over the CHICKEN and drip the remaining BUTTER on the bird.

10. Slice 1 TABLEspoon of UNMELTED BUTTER and place it inside the CHICKEN CAVITY.

11. Measure ½ TEAspoon of SEA SALT. Take a pinch between your fingers and liberally sprinkle the SALT over the CHICKEN. Continue until out of SALT.

12. Take sharp knife and chop up ROSEMARY, SAGE and THYME on the cutting board. This is a rough estimate, but 3 sprigs of each herb will get you the 2 TABLEspoons you need. (Note: If you find yourself singing Simon & Garfunkel tunes right about now, that's totally normal)

13. Sprinkle ROSEMARY, SAGE and THYME over the entire CHICKEN.

14. Place 1 sprig of ROSEMARY, SAGE and THYME inside CHICKEN CAVITY.
15. Look at CHICKEN PACKAGING to determine how much the bird weighs.
16. Do the math to determine how many minutes you need to cook the chicken. Remember: 20 minutes per pound!
17. Put on oven mitts. Open oven door. Slide out rack.
18. Place baking dish on rack. Slide in rack. Close oven door. Take off oven mitts.
19. Set oven timer for just half the time you computed.
20. Measure 4 TABLEspoons of BUTTER and add to small plate #2. This is the butter to go with the bread at dinner.
21. Put colander in sink.
22. Wash TOMATOES. Pat dry with paper towels.
23. Slice ¼ of BREAD. Add 1 slice to each dinner plate.
24. Open BAG OF SALAD. Add SALAD to salad bowls.
25. Slice TOMATOES. Throw out TOPS and BOTTOMS of TOMATOES.
26. Run WATER in sink. Rinse off icky, green SEEDS from TOMATOES. Then, drop TOMATOES into colander to dry.
27. When the oven timer goes off, put on oven mitts. Open oven door. Slide out rack.
28. Place baking dish on stovetop burners.
29. Grab baster. Suck up JUICES on bottom of baking dish. Squeeze out JUICES all over CHICKEN to tenderize the bird.
30. Return baking dish to rack.
31. Slide in rack. Close oven door. Take off oven mitts.
32. Set oven timer for 10 minutes LESS than the time you need to complete cooking.
33. Add TOMATOES to salad bowls.
34. When oven timer goes off, open TAKE-N-BAKE BREAD.
35. Put on oven mitts. Open oven door. Slide out bottom rack.
36. Place BREAD on bottom rack. Slide in rack. Close oven door. Take off oven mitts.
37. When oven timer goes off, put on oven mitt. Open oven door. Slide out rack.
38. Place baking dish on stovetop burners.
39. Slide in rack. Close oven door. Take off oven mitts.
40. Stick instant-read meat thermometer into a BREAST. The temperature must be 160 degrees or Ms. Right Now might die.
41. If the temperature is 160 or higher, the chicken is done. But if the temperature is lower than 160, return the baking dish back to the oven for 5 minutes.

42. Once the CHICKEN is done, re-set oven timer for 5 minutes. Turn up oven's heat to 500 degrees. This is to finish cooking the BREAD.
43. Rip top of BAG OF RICE as instructed. Cook in microwave for 90 seconds.
44. Use baster to squeeze JUICES all over CHICKEN.
45. Ask Ms. Right Now if she prefers white meat (Breast and Wings) or dark meat (Legs and Thighs).
46. When RICE is done, remove bag and tear off top. This mofo is hot!
47. Add SALAD DRESSING to salads.
48. Pour half the RICE onto each dinner plate.
49. When timer goes off, turn off oven.
50. Put on oven mitt. Open oven door. Slide out bottom rack.
51. Remove BREAD and place on cutting board.
52. Slide in rack. Close oven door. Take off oven mitt.
53. Slice CHICKEN. Place two pieces of whichever MEAT she likes on her dinner plate. Do the same for yours.
54. Carry butter plate and salad bowls to table.
55. Slice ¼ Loaf of BREAD. Put 2 SLICES on each dinner plate.
56. Carry dinner plates to table.
57. Dinner is served!

Three Cooks' Chicken Divan to Die For

The talents of two people and the idiocy of one person combined to create a Chicken Dee-Vahn unlike any other in creation.

The original recipe came from Donna Franklin, the Kitchen Goddess who gave me 25 recipes. But after I tried Chicken Divan the first time, I remembered Steve Egan's dad making a similar dish for us on a trip to the DC area. So I asked for Frank Egan's take on this meal. You can thank him for the cheese!

And you can thank my culinary cluelessness for the ease of cooking.

Donna's original recipe started like this: Mix soup, mayo, and cream. Put a thin layer of sauce on the bottom of a 9 x 13 pan. Spread a layer of noodles…

So, that's what I did. An hour later, it smelled delicious, but something wasn't right.

In the middle of the pan, everything was gooey goodness. Strangely – to me, anyway – not all the noodles at the edges of the pan got cooked. In fact, some of the noodles became *harder* than they had been before I put the pan in the oven.

Confused, I emailed Donna to see where I'd goofed. I am very happy I didn't call her; she wouldn't have had time to recover from her hysterical laughing.

She emailed back, "Oh, Jamie…I should have been clearer in the directions. You have to cook the noodles first before adding them to the pan." Every female on earth would have known that instinctively. Yet another example, fellas, of why guys like us need a book like this!

Despite my total humiliation, I realized I was on to something. I mean, 75% of the noodles got cooked in the pan. The others suffered from a lack of moisture. Solution: add more liquid! Amazingly, it worked.

This is a lot of food, so you'll have at least two nights' worth of leftovers.

Ease: 2 Chefs
Cost: $56
Preparation Time: 15 minutes
Cooking Time: 45 minutes

Ingredients:
Tyson Pre-cooked Chicken Breast Strips (not breaded) – 1 package; $8.99
Frozen Broccoli – 2 ten-ounce packages; $2.69 each
Egg Noodles – 4 cups; $1.39 per box
Cream of Chicken Soup – 3 cans; $1.69 each
Mayonnaise - 1 cup; $3.00 per jar
Half & Half – 1/2 cup; $1.89 (Found in the dairy aisle next to the Heavy Creams)
Lemon Juice – 1 TEAspoon; $1.00 per 4-ounce bottle
Shredded Cheddar Cheese – 1 Cup; $3.39 per bag
Italian Bread Crumbs – 2 Cups; $1.89
Sea Salt; $3.99
Pre-washed Salad – 1 Bag; $5
Tomatoes – 2; $2.99
Salad Dressing – Bottle of your choice; $2
Take-n-Bake Bread – 1 Loaf; $2.00 (*Available in Bakery section of supermarket*)
Butter – 4 TABLEspoons; $5.50 per package of four sticks

Recommended Wine: Merlot or, if feeling adventurous, Syrah

Tools, etc:
Measuring Cup
Mixing Bowl
Measuring Spoons
Can Opener
Large Baking Dish
Wooden Spoon
Oven Mitt
Small Plate
Cutting Board
Colander (the thingy with all the holes; it's for draining pasta)
Instant-Read Meat Thermometer

Directions:
1. Measure ½ Cup of HALF AND HALF and add to the mixing bowl.

1. Measure 1 Cup of MAYONNAISE and add to mixing bowl.
2. Open 3 Cans of CREAM OF CHICKEN SOUP and add to mixing bowl. Cream of Chicken is the circus car of soups – you'll be amazed by how much stays in the bottom of the can. Use a spoon to scoop it all out.
3. Rinse out the CANS you just emptied and chuck them in your recycling bin. Remember, Ms. Right Now wants you to A.B.R. – Always Be Recycling!
4. Measure ¼ TEAspoon of LEMON JUICE and add to mixing bowl.
5. Mix INGREDIENTS in mixing bowl. Be careful, it's messy.
6. Use wooden spoon to spread a thin layer of SAUCE over every inch of the large baking dish. It's tough to specify how much sauce to use, so imagine you're spreading tomato sauce on a pizza crust.
7. Place UNCOOKED NOODLES evenly across the bottom of the dish.
8. Open 2 packages of BROCCOLI and spread evenly on top of the noodles.
9. Place the CHICKEN STRIPS on top of the BROCCOLI. Lay down the CHICKEN like you were laying down 2x4's when building a deck.
10. Pre-heat oven to 375 degrees.
11. Pour rest of SAUCE all over the CHICKEN. Be sure to drench the edges.
12. Measure 1 Cup of CHEDDAR CHEESE and use your fingers to spread the cheese evenly on top of CHICKEN.
13. Cover everything with ITALIAN BREADCRUMBS. You are freelancing, here, so go crazy. Make sure the entire surface has some crumbs on it.
14. Put on oven mitt. Open oven door. Slide out rack.
15. Place baking dish on rack. Slide in rack. Close door.
16. Set oven timer for 35 minutes.
17. Cut 4 TABLEspoons of BUTTER (Use the ruler on the wax paper wrapper to measure this) and put BUTTER on small plate for later.
18. Place colander in sink.
19. Wash TOMATOES. Dry TOMATOES with paper towel.
20. Slice TOMATOES on plate. Throw out TOPS and BOTTOMS of tomatoes.
21. Run water in sink. Rinse icky, green SEEDS off. Then, drop TOMATOS into colander to dry.
22. Open SALAD BAG. Put SALAD into salad bowls.
23. When oven timer goes off, re-set oven timer for 10 minutes.
24. Open TAKE-N-BAKE BREAD.
25. Put on oven mitt. Open oven door. Slide out bottom rack.

26. Place BREAD on bottom rack. Slide in rack. Close oven door. Take off oven mitt.
27. When oven timer goes off, put on oven mitt. Open oven door. Slide out top rack.
28. Place baking dish on stovetop burners.
29. Slide in rack. Close oven door. Take off oven mitt.
30. Stick instant-read meat thermometer into a BREAST. The temperature must be 160 degrees or Ms. Right Now might die.
31. If the temperature is 160 or higher, the chicken is done. But if the temperature is lower than 160, return the baking dish back to the oven for 5 minutes.
32. Once the CHICKEN is done, re-set oven timer for 5 minutes. Turn up oven's heat to 500 degrees. This is to finish cooking the BREAD.
33. Add TOMATOES to salad bowls.
34. Add SALAD DRESSING.
35. Carry salad bowls and butter plate out to table.
36. When oven timer goes off, turn off oven.
37. Put on oven mitt. Open oven door. Slide out bottom rack.
38. Remove BREAD and place on cutting board.
39. Slide in rack. Close oven door. Take off oven mitt.
40. Use spatula to cut and move CHICKEN DIVAN servings onto dinner plates.
41. Slice ¼ Loaf of BREAD. Put 2 SLICES on each dinner plate.
42. Carry dinner plates out to table.
43. Dinner is served!

Jones's Baked Chicken with Onion Rings

Tracy Jones's Mom has got it going on.
   What this recipe lacks in a zippy title, it makes up for with the amazing aroma that will fill your apartment.
   Tracy is a sexy physical therapist, which means after she cooks you a great meal she can then help work out any, uh, kinks you have.

Ease: 2 Chefs
Cost: $51
Preparation Time: 5 minutes
Cooking Time: 60 minutes

Ingredients:
Thawed Chicken breasts – 6; $8 for 12 frozen breasts

Sour Cream – 16-ounce container; $1-3, depending on brand
Cream of Mushroom Soup – 1 can; $1.69
Dried Onion Rings – 1 small can; $2.49 (*These are found in the aisle with canned vegetables, probably near jars of artichokes*)
Sea Salt – ½ TABLEspoon; $3.99
Cracked Black Pepper; ½ TABLEspoon; $3.99
Paprika – ½ TABLEspoon; $2.39
Butter – 8 TABLEspoons "divided"; $5.50 for four sticks (*"Divided" means the ingredients will be used at separate steps in the process*)
Herb Rice – 1 Microwavable Bag; $2.49
Pre-made Salad; $5.00
Tomatoes – 4; $2.99 per pound
Salad Dressing – 1 bottle of your choice; $2.00
Take-n-Bake Bread – 1 Loaf; $2.00 (*Found in Bakery section of supermarket*)
Non-Stick Spray – $4.99

Recommended Wine: Cabernet or, if feeling adventurous, Petite Sirah

Tools, etc:
Large Plates – 3
Measuring Spoons
Large Baking Dish
Small Plate
Oven Mitt – 2
Paring Knife
Mixing Bowl
Instant-Read Meat Thermometer
Large Spoon
Cutting Board
Colander
Can Opener

Directions:

1. Spread out CHICKEN BREASTS on two large plates.

2. Pre-heat oven to 350 degrees.

3. Spray baking dish with NON-STICK SPRAY.

4. Measure 1 TABLEspoon of SEA SALT.

5. Take pinch of SEA SALT and sprinkle all over one side of one CHICKEN BREAST. Repeat for remaining CHICKEN BREASTS.

6. Measure 1 TABLEspoon of BLACK PEPPER.

7. Take pinch of BLACK PEPPER and sprinkle all over one side of one CHICKEN BREAST. Repeat for remaining CHICKEN BREASTS.

8. Measure 1 TABLEspoon of SEA SALT.

9. Take pinch of PAPRIKA and sprinkle all over one side of one CHICKEN BREAST. Repeat for remaining CHICKEN BREASTS.
10. Flip over CHICKEN BREASTS.
11. Repeat steps 4-9 for each BREAST.
12. Place the BREASTS in the baking dish.
13. Cut 6 tablespoons of BUTTER (Use the ruler on the wax paper wrapper to measure) and place 1 TABLEspoon on each CHICKEN BREAST.
14. Place remaining 2 TABLEspoons of BUTTER on small plate.
15. Put on oven mitts. Open oven door. Slide out rack.
16. Place baking dish on rack. Slide in rack. Close door.
17. Set oven timer for 45 minutes.
18. Empty 16 ounces of SOUR CREAM into mixing bowl.
19. Pour SOUP into mixing bowl. Mix CONTENTS thoroughly.
20. Set mixing bowl on counter next to stovetop.
21. Wash TOMATOES. Pat dry with paper towels.
22. Place colander in sink.
23. On cutting board, slice TOMATOES. Throw out both the tops and bottoms of TOMATOES.
24. Turn on WATER in sink. Take SLICED TOMATOES in your fingers and rinse off the icky, green SEEDS.
25. Drop clean TOMATOES into colander to dry.
26. Open SALAD BAG. Add SALAD to two salad bowls.
27. Slice ITALIAN BREAD and place 1 slice on both dinner plates.
28. When oven timer goes off, put on oven mitts. Open oven door and slide out rack.
29. Take out baking dish and place it on the stovetop burners. Close oven door. Take off oven mitts.
30. Grab a large plate. Take a fork and stack each of the BREASTS on the large plate.
31. Pour the SOUP and SOUR CREAM MIXTURE into the baking dish.
32. Mix it up with the hot, buttery SAUCE in the bottom of the baking dish.
33. Return BREASTS to the baking dish.
34. Use spoon to totally cover BREASTS in SAUCE (yes, you can snicker).
35. Open CAN OF ONION RINGS. Using your fingers, sprinkle ONION RINGS all over BREASTS and exposed areas of the baking dish.
36. Put on oven mitts and open oven door. Slide out rack. Place baking dish on rack. Slide in rack. Close door.

37. Set oven timer for 15 minutes.
38. When the oven timer goes off, turn off oven. Put on oven mitts.
39. Open oven door. Slide out rack. Place baking dish on stovetop burners.
40. Stick instant-read meat thermometer into a BREAST. The temperature must be 160 degrees or Ms. Right Now might die.
41. If the temperature is 160 or higher, the chicken is done. But if the temperature is lower than 160, return the baking dish back to the oven for 5 minutes.
42. Once the CHICKEN is done, grab BAG of MICROWAVABLE RICE. Open sides of top as instructed.
43. Put BAG in microwave and cook for 90 seconds.
44. Add SALAD DRESSING to SALADS.
45. When RICE is done, remove bag and tear off top. Be careful, this mofo is hot!
46. Carry butter plate and salad bowls to table.
47. Pour half the RICE onto each dinner plate.
48. Place 1 BREAST on each dinner plate. Use spoon to cover the BREAST with SAUCE.
49. Carry the dinner plates to the table.
50. Dinner is served!

Laurence's "Love Chicken"

a.k.a. Quick Roast Chicken with reduction

As a movie producer, Laurence Rosenthal discovered the script for "Scream." As a screenwriting instructor, he oversaw the writing of the first screenplay I ever sold. Moral of the story? LR can recognize talent <u>and</u> make lemonade from lemons. He can also cook the bejesus out of some bird.

    This recipe would scare most people with kitchen experience. See, "reduction" is a frightening word. I am willing to bet that your mom has not attempted any recipes requiring reduction. And if your mom hasn't tried it, then Ms. Right Now's mom probably hasn't, either. Which means your date definitely hasn't.

    But there's no reason to be scared. Basically, reduction is – and I never thought I'd use this phrase in my life – a really cool science experiment.

    You're gonna have tons of leftovers, too.

    The only sticking point is you have to buy a cast iron skillet, which isn't a cooking tool you'll use every day. But, as Laurence so eloquently put it, "The motherfucker is extremely heavy. It can be used an as agent of death." Home invaders beware!

    Ease: 2 Chefs
    Cost: $52
    Preparation Time: 20 minutes (not including thawing the chicken!)

Cooking Time: 60 minutes

Ingredients:
One Whole Chicken (3-4 pounds); $12.99
Sea Salt – ½ TEAspoon; $3.99
Cracked Black Pepper – ½ TEAspoon; $3.99
Shallots – 3; $2.99 per pound (*Shallots are little, purple onion-like guys, found near onions in the supermarket*)
Vermouth – 1 Cup; $8 per bottle
Brown Rice – 1 Microwavable Bag; $2.49
Salad – 1 Bag pre-washed; $5
Tomatoes – 2; $2.99 per pound
Salad Dressing – Bottle of your choice; $2
Take-n-Bake Bread – 1 Loaf; $2.00 (*Found in Bakery section of supermarket*)
Non-Stick Spray; $4.99

Wine Recommendation: Cabernet or, if feeling adventurous, Sangiovese

Tools, etc:
Cast Iron Skillet – 12 inch; $27. *This will probably come "pre-seasoned." I do not know how they manage to do that, but just go with it.*
Paper Towels
Measuring Spoons
Oven Mitts
Measuring Cup
Cutting Board
Sharp Knife
Large Plate
Wooden Spoon
Barbeque Fork – Large
Barbeque Tongs - Large
Colander (the thingy with all the holes; it's for draining things)
Instant-Read Meat Thermometer

Directions:

1. Thaw CHICKEN!

2. Open oven door. Peek inside. See any dark brown, crusty stuff on the bottom or sides? I am willing to bet you've got at least a dozen rock solid drippings from frozen pizzas of dinners past. Pray you have a "self-cleaning" oven. If so, press the button. This will usually take 2 hours, so plan accordingly. If you don't have a self-cleaning oven…loosen up that elbow, dude! Soak the sponge and scrub the hell out of that oven. This is vital because, as my lungs painfully discovered, when you crank the oven to 500 degrees everything smokes inside that bad boy. Walking into a smoky apartment might make Ms. Right Now drop to her knees, but not in a good way.

3. Once you've cleaned the oven, use paper towels to dry the inside.

4. Pre-heat oven to 500 degrees.

5. Wash CHICKEN under cold water in sink. Dry CHICKEN with paper towels. This will take @ 5 minutes. Be sure to wash faucet knob afterwards because it'll be GROSS from your fingers getting slimy after handling the chicken.
6. Spray cast iron skillet with PAM.
7. Place CHICKEN on its back in the cast iron skillet. (Hint: Its LEGS should be pointing up at you)
8. Measure ½ TEAspoon of SEA SALT.
9. Take a pinch between your fingers and liberally sprinkle all over the CHICKEN. Continue until out of SALT.
10. Make sure SALT is clearly visible all over the bird. If not, add more.
11. Measure ½ TEAspoon of BLACK PEPPER.
12. Take a pinch between your fingers and liberally sprinkle all over the CHICKEN. Continue until out of PEPPER.
13. Make sure PEPPER is clearly visible all over the bird. If not, add more.
14. Amazingly, that's all the seasoning you need to do for now. The chicken will cook wonderfully in its own juices.
15. Put on oven mitts. Open oven door. Slide out oven rack.
16. Place skillet on rack. Slide rack in. Close door.
17. Set oven timer for 30 minutes.
18. Place colander in sink.
19. Open SALAD and add to salad bowls.
20. Measure 1 cup of VERMOUTH and set aside for later.
21. Place cutting board on counter.
22. You now have to slice the SHALLOTS. I don't care how macho you are. Maybe you didn't even cry when Old Yeller died. You will cry when slicing shallots, unless you follow this direction.
23. Take a dinner spoon and suck on it. Seriously.
24. Peel 2 layers off the first SHALLOT.
25. Using the sharp knife, slice SHALLOT lengthwise into 6-7 strips. Then, slice the strips in half. Repeat for the other two shallots.
26. Furiously scrub hands with DISH SOAP. Shallots will stink up your cuticles, and that won't go over well later when you try to feed her dessert.
27. Rinse off cutting board.
28. When timer goes off, put on oven mitts.
29. Stop! That skillet is really fucking hot! A cast iron skillet is used because it is a fantastic conductor of heat at any temperature. So, think about how good a conductor it'll be at 500

degrees Fahrenheit. You might want to grab a dishtowel and wrap that around your power hand, too.

30. Open oven door. Slide out oven rack. Remember, the skillet weighs 20 pounds.
31. Grab skillet and place it on the front stovetop burners. Make sure the skillet handle points away from your belt buckle. (You don't want to accidentally tip it over)
32. Slide in rack. Close oven door.
33. Sizzle. Pop. Hear that? Welcome to Splatter City. You are now ready to execute "The Flip Over" which is the Mary Lou Retton of chicken maneuvers. Stick it!
34. Take off oven mitts.
35. Grab large barbeque fork in your power hand and the barbeque tongs in your other hand.
36. Stick fork deep into power hand side of the CHICKEN.
37. Insert tongs into the hole in the front of the chicken. Take deep breath.
38. Lift CHICKEN and turn it onto its CHEST. (Hint: Now the legs should be pointing away from you)
39. Measure ½ TEAspoon of SEA SALT. Take a pinch between your fingers and liberally sprinkle all over the CHICKEN. Continue until out of SALT.
40. Make sure SALT is clearly visible all over the bird. If not, add more.
41. Measure ½ TEAspoon of BLACK PEPPER. Take a pinch between your fingers and liberally sprinkle all over the CHICKEN. Continue until out of PEPPER.
42. Make sure PEPPER is clearly visible all over the bird. If not, add more.
43. Put on oven mitts. Open door. Slide out rack.
44. Place skillet on rack. Slide rack in. Close door.
45. Set oven timer for 20 minutes.
46. Wash TOMATOES. Pat dry with paper towels.
47. Put colander in sink.
48. Slice ¼ loaf of ITALIAN BREAD. Add 1 slice to each dinner plate.
49. Open BAG OF SALAD. Add SALAD to salad bowls.
50. Slice TOMATOES. Throw out TOPS and BOTTOMS of TOMATOES.
51. Run WATER in sink. Rinse off icky, green SEEDS from TOMATOES. Then, drop TOMATOES into colander to dry.
52. When oven timer goes off, open TAKE-N-BAKE BREAD.
53. Put on oven mitt. Open oven door. Slide out bottom rack.
54. Place BREAD on bottom rack. Slide in rack. Close oven door. Take off oven mitt.
55. Reset oven timer for 10 minutes.

56. When oven timer goes off, turn off oven. Put on oven mitts.
57. Stop! That skillet is even fucking hotter! You might want to grab a dishtowel and wrap that around your power hand, too.
58. Open oven door. Slide out oven rack. Remember, the skillet still weighs 20 pounds.
59. Grab skillet and place it on the front right stovetop burners. Make sure the skillet handle points away to the right of your belt buckle. (You still don't want to accidentally tip it over)
60. Slide in rack. Close oven door. Remove oven mitts.
61. Stick instant-read meat thermometer into a BREAST. The temperature must be 160 degrees or Ms. Right Now may die.
62. If the temperature is 160 or higher, the chicken is done. But if the temperature is lower than 160, return the baking dish back to the oven for 5 minutes.
63. Once CHICKEN is done, place large plate on burner left of skillet.
64. Grab large barbeque fork in your power hand and the barbeque tongs in your other hand.
65. Stick fork deep into power hand side of the CHICKEN.
66. Insert tongs into the hole in the front of the chicken. Take deep breath.
67. Lift CHICKEN and place onto large plate. Now, bow to the adoring crowd.
68. This next part is where you will cement your legend, sir.
69. Look at all the yummy GREASE and DRIPPINGS in the skillet.
70. Turn on the burner flame under the skillet to a medium-high heat (Here's the easy way to tell what is high, medium, low and all the inbetweens: squat down, and crank the flame. See how high that is? Okay, that's HIGH. Now lower it all the way till it's just above almost blowing out. That is LOW. Now, raise the flame till it's in the middle of high and low – that's medium. So, "medium-high" is somewhere between that current flame and high)
71. Add the SLICED CHALLOTS to the skillet.
72. Using the wooden spoon, scrape up the BURNT ON STUFF at the bottom of the skillet. Be careful not to create huge balls of burnt stuff.
73. Spread out the ingredients across the skillet.
74. When the CHALLOTS become golden or translucent, add the cup of VERMOUTH.
75. Beware the dreaded "Stovetop Lean." You know how "experienced" pool tables lean more to one side than the other? Old stovetops can do the same thing, causing the contents of frying pans to fill higher on one side. This is a potential nuclear disaster waiting to happen. Pay attention to your frying pan! You might have to jury rig a spoon on one side to balance things out. Do NOT use anything flammable to do the balancing.
76. Crank the flame to high.
77. Stir continuously with the wooden spoon. The LIQUID in the skillet will gradually evaporate, leaving behind a thicker substance. This is called "reducing the liquid." Too bad high school science projects never smelled this good.

78. When the mixture becomes the consistency of GRAVY, turn off flame.
79. Spoon the REDUCTION over the chicken. (Ms. Right Now may "service" you right then and there, so be ready for it!)
80. Put on oven mitt. Open oven door. Slide out bottom rack.
81. Remove BREAD and place on cutting board.
82. Slide in rack. Close oven door. Take off oven mitt.
83. Rip top of BAG OF RICE as instructed. Cook in microwave for 90 seconds.
84. Slice ¼ Loaf of BREAD. Put 2 SLICES on each dinner plate.
85. Ask her if she prefers white meat (Breast and Wings) or dark meat (Legs and Thighs).
86. Carve CHICKEN accordingly and serve onto dinner plates.
87. Add TOMATOES to salad bowls.
88. When RICE is done, remove bag and tear off top. Be careful, this mofo is hot!
89. Add SALAD DRESSING to salads.
90. Carry butter plate and salad bowls to table.
91. Pour half the RICE onto each dinner plate.
92. Carry dinner plates to table.
93. Dinner is served!

Kleiman's Rosemary Brewed Chicken

You don't know it, but you've seen Mark Kleiman's work. A film editor extraordinaire, Kleims has cut video for many Super Bowl and World Series telecasts. He's kind of a big deal.

Why wasn't I surprised that a Milwaukee native devised an easy chicken recipe that uses *beer*?

This meal is great at home – in this example you'll learn how to finish it in a frying pan. But you can also finish it on the grill – score big points at a tailgater, too – by adding barbeque sauce instead of the olive oil mixture.

The key to this recipe is making the marinade the **day before** you eat, and letting the chicken soak overnight in the fridge. The chicken will taste pretty good if you rush it all, but it will be ten times better if you follow the pre-cooking instructions. So, you'll need to plan ahead, brother.

Ease: 3 Chefs
Cost: $54
Preparation Time: 24 hours
Cooking Time: 7 minutes on date night

Ingredients:
Skinless Chicken Thighs – 1 package; $9.99

Coca-Cola – 2 Cans; $1
Beer – 4 Cans; $3. *Doesn't matter what brand, so don't waste the good stuff.*
Yellow Onion – 1; 99 cents per pound
Minced Garlic – 1.5 TEAspoons; $2.49
Rosemary – 2 TABLEspoons; $2.99
Olive Oil – 3 TABLEspoons; $6-13 per bottle
Paprika – handful; $2.39
Brown Rice – 1 Microwavable Bag; $2.49
Salad – 1 Bag pre-washed; $5
Tomatoes – 2; $2.99 per pound
Salad Dressing – Bottle of your choice; $2
Take-n-Bake Bread – 1 Loaf; $2.00 (*Found in Bakery section of supermarket*)
Butter – 4 TABLEspoons; $5.50 per 4 sticks

Wine Recommendation: Merlot or, if feeling adventurous, Barbera D' Alba

Tools, etc:
Pasta Pot – 4 quart
Frying Pan – Large
Paper Towels
Sharp Knife
Measuring Spoons
Wooden Spoon
Barbeque Tongs – Large
Small Plate
Colander (the thingy with all the holes; it's for draining things)
Cutting Board
Stopwatch
Instant-Read Meat Thermometer

Directions:

You should – but don't have to – execute the next **18 DIRECTIONS 1 day prior to** your date.

1. Thaw CHICKEN.
2. Wash CHICKEN under cold water in sink. Dry CHICKEN with paper towels. This will take @ 5 minutes. Be sure to wash faucet knob afterwards because it'll be GROSS from your fingers getting slimy after handling the chicken.
3. Peel 2 layers off ONION. Then, use sharp knife to dice ONION into pieces the size of onions on a Micky D's hamburger.
4. Furiously wash hands with DISH SOAP. Onion will stink up your cuticles, and that won't go over well later when you try to feed her dessert.
5. Place pasta pot onto a stovetop burner.
6. Pour 2 cans of COKE into pasta pot. Pour 4 cans of BEER into pasta pot.
7. Measure 1 TEAspoon of MINCED GARLIC and add to pasta pot.

8. Measure 1 TABLEspoon of ROSEMARY and add to pasta pot.
9. On the cutting board chop off both ends of the YELLOW ONION. Then, cut the REMAINDER in half.
10. Remove ONION SKIN and 1 layer of ONION. Throw out skin and layer.
11. You now have a halved yellow onion that has been cut on two sides.
12. Turn ONION so that 1 cut side faces you. Choose 1 UNCUT SIDE.
13. Slice along that uncut side. You are trying to cut pieces the size of the onions on a Mickey D's hamburger.
14. Add DICED ONION to pasta pot.
15. Rinse off cutting board.
16. Furiously scrub hands with DISH SOAP. ONION will stink up your cuticles, which won't go over well later when you try to feed her dessert.
17. Use barbeque tongs to carefully place CHICKEN in pasta pot.
18. Stir MIXTURE with tongs. Cover pot.
19. Crank burner flame to high.
20. Rinse out the CANS you just emptied and chuck them in your recycling bin. Remember, Ms. Right Now wants you to A.B.R. – Always Be Recycling!
21. Wash tongs in sink – you're gonna need them tomorrow.
22. Once liquid has started to boil, lower flame to low-medium. (That's in-between low and medium, just so you know).
23. Now, the mixture should be simmering. Cover pasta pot but leave a little crack for air.
24. Set oven timer for 45 minutes.
25. When oven timer goes off, turn off flame. Move pasta pot to a cold burner.
26. Set timer for 120 minutes.
27. When timer goes off, move pasta pot into fridge. (This may require your learning how to adjust the shelves in your refrigerator, but that's a lifelong skill.)
28. 20 minutes prior to eating, pre-heat oven to 350 degrees. This is for the BREAD.
29. Set oven timer for 5 minutes.
30. When oven timer goes off, open TAKE-N-BAKE BREAD.
31. Put on oven mitt. Open oven door. Slide out rack.
32. Place BREAD on rack. Slide in rack. Close oven door. Take off oven mitt.
33. Set oven timer for 15 minutes.
34. Wash TOMATOES. Pat dry with paper towels.
35. Slice 4 TABLEspoons of BUTTER and place on small plate for later.

36. Put colander in sink.
37. Open BAG OF SALAD. Add SALAD to salad bowls.
38. Slice TOMATOES on cutting board. Throw out TOPS and BOTTOMS of TOMATOES.
39. Run WATER in sink. Rinse off icky, green SEEDS from TOMATOES. Then, drop TOMATOES into colander to dry.
40. Remove CHICKEN from broth. Place CHICKEN on spare plate. (If you don't have a garbage disposal in your sink, it's not a bad idea to dump out the pasta pot broth in the toilet. Seriously. All those rosemary stems will be a royal pain in the ass – so to speak – to clean out of your drain. Just flush 'em bye-bye.)
41. When oven timer goes off, turn off oven.
42. Put on oven mitt. Open oven door. Slide out bottom rack.
43. Remove BREAD and place on cutting board.
44. Slide in rack. Close oven door. Take off oven mitt.
45. Place large frying pan on stovetop burner.
46. Measure 3 TABLEspoons OLIVE OIL and add to frying pan.
47. Measure ½ teaspoon MINCED GARLIC and add to frying pan.
48. Measure 1 TABLEspoon ROSEMARY and add to frying pan.
49. Grab PAPRIKA. Lightly sprinkle PAPRIKA on the face-up side of CHICKEN.
50. Turn on flame under frying pan to low-medium.
51. Use wooden spoon to stir the MIXTURE until OLIVE OIL starts to pop.
52. Beware the dreaded "Stovetop Lean." You know how "experienced" pool tables lean more to one side than the other? Old stovetops can do the same thing, causing the contents of frying pans to fill higher on one side. This is a potential nuclear disaster waiting to happen. Pay attention to your frying pan! You might have to jury rig a spoon on one side to balance things out. Do NOT use anything flammable to do the balancing.
53. Use tongs to place CHICKEN in frying pan.
54. Use wooden spoon to coat the top of CHICKEN with the frying pan MIXTURE.
55. Set oven timer for 3 minutes.
56. Add TOMATOES to salad bowls.
57. When oven timer goes off, use tongs to flip CHICKEN onto other side.
58. Re-set oven timer for 3 minutes.
59. When oven timer goes off, turn off flame. Use tongs to move CHICKEN onto clean plates.
60. Stick instant-read meat thermometer into a BREAST. The temperature must be 160 degrees or Ms. Right Now might die.

61. If the temperature is 160 or higher, the chicken is done. But if the temperature is lower than 160, return the baking dish back to the oven for 5 minutes.
62. Once the CHICKEN is done, rip top of BAG OF RICE according to directions. Cook in microwave for 90 seconds.
63. Re-coat CHICKEN with MIXTURE.
64. Slice ¼ Loaf of BREAD. Put 2 SLICES on each dinner plate.
65. When RICE is done, remove bag and tear off top. Be careful, this mofo is hot!
66. Add SALAD DRESSING to SALADS.
67. Use tongs to place CHICKEN on dinner plates.
68. Pour half the RICE onto each dinner plate.
69. Carry butter plate and salad bowls to table.
70. Carry dinner plates to table.
71. Dinner is served!

Cleaning-wise, do yourself a favor and dump *frying pan* CONTENTS into *sink*. Then, fill *frying pan* **halfway** with WATER, place on *stovetop burner* and heat to a boil. Let it boil for a few minutes to loosen up any burnt or sticky remnants. You'll thank god you did this whenever you eventually try to wash the pan.

Synor's Black Bean Chicken Chili

A.B. Synor is a world-class connoisseur of food and drink, so when he offered a recipe I jumped all over it.

Besides being tasty, this meal is huge and freezable; even if you just cook it for yourself, you'll have four dinners waiting for you down the road.

Ease: 3 Chefs
Cost: $61 (This is deceiving; $28 of it is oil and seasonings you'll use again and again)
Preparation Time: 20 minutes (not including thawing the chicken!)
Cooking Time: 30 minutes

Ingredients:
Tyson's Boneless, skinless Diced Chicken Breasts; $8.99. *You can buy regular Chicken Breasts, cook them and chop them up yourself, if you want, but why would you want?*
Red Bell Peppers – 2; $3.99 per pound
White Onion – 1; $1.29 per pound
Garlic Powder – 2 TEAspoons; $6.29. *Important not to add 2 TABLEspoons, like I did the first time. See? This is why I write out the entire thing, rather than using abbreviations!*
Extra Virgin Olive Oil – 3 TABLEspoons; $6-13
Chili Powder – ¼ Cup; $6.69

Ground Cumin – 2 TEAspoons; $7.39
Black Beans – two 15-ounce Cans; $1.29 per can
Stewed Tomatoes – one 28-ounce Can; $1.29
Beer – 1 Cup
Shredded Sharp Cheddar Cheese – one 15-ounce bag; $3.79
White Rice – 1 Microwavable Bag; $2.49
Salad – 1 Bag pre-washed; $5
Tomatoes – 2; $2.99 per pound
Salad Dressing – Bottle of your choice; $2
Oyster Crackers – 1 box; $3.00 *Some people like to crush crackers into their chili. God forbid you don't have them if she's one of the crushers!*

Wine Recommendation: Zinfandel or, if feeling adventurous, Grenache (which is pronounced gren-ash)

Tools, etc:
Paper Towels
Large Pasta Pot
Sharp Knife
Cutting Board
Measuring Spoons
Measuring Cup
Sauce Pot
Wooden Spoon
Colander (the thingy with all the holes; it's for draining things)
Bowls – 4

Directions:

1. Wash RED PEPPERS. Pat dry with paper towels.
2. Put large pasta pot on stovetop burner.
3. Measure and add 3 tablespoons of OLIVE OIL to large pasta pot.
4. Add CHICKEN CHUNKS to large pasta pot.
5. Take knife and cut out the STEM on the RED BELL PEPPERS. Throw away STEMS.
6. Next, cut open the PEPPERS above the trash. Shake out all SEEDS. Cut out AND throw out all WHITE STUFF inside peppers.
7. On the cutting board, dice PEPPERS into 1/8" x 1/8" pieces, a.k.a. the size of McDonald's Hamburger onions.
8. Add PEPPERS to large pasta pot.
9. If you don't want to cry while chopping ONIONS, take a dinner spoon and suck on it. Seriously.
10. On the cutting board, chop off both ends of the WHITE ONION. Then, cut the REMAINDER in half.

11. Remove SKIN and throw the skin in the trash. I like to remove the second layer, too, just to be safe.
12. You now have a halved white onion that has been cut on two sides.
13. Turn ONION so that 1 cut side faces you. Choose 1 UNCUT SIDE.
14. Thinly slice along that uncut side. Place ONION in measuring cup. You want ½ Cup of sliced onions. The point here is to slice the onion as thinly as possible. Think of it like a wet t-shirt contest, only instead of "Skin to Win!" this motto is, "Thin to Win!"
15. Dice ONION into 1/8" x 1/8" pieces.
16. Add ONION to large pasta pot.
17. Repeat steps 13 – 16 with the other half of the onion.
18. Furiously scrub hands with dish soap. ONION will stink up your cuticles, which won't go over well later when you try to feed her dessert.
19. Measure and add 4 teaspoons of GARLIC POWDER to large frying pan.
20. Turn on flame beneath large pasta pot to medium heat.
21. Set oven timer for 8 minutes. This will get the chicken to the point that it's almost cooked. Stir CHICKEN frequently.
22. You now have to measure the CUMIN and CHILI POWDER. WAIT! It is quite tricky to get the exact amount you need. Follow these instructions carefully or you'll be kicking up cumin/chili powder dust for days. Ahh-choo!
23. Unscrew the top to the CHILI POWDER. Gently remove the plastic thing. You are doing this because it'll take forever getting the clumps of powder through the holes.
24. Throw out the plastic thing. You don't need it and it's a lot of fun to chuck stuff the food corporations force on us!
25. Gently shake out ¼ cup of CHILI POWDER into the measuring cup. Screw on top.
26. Unscrew the top to the CUMIN (Important note: this is pronounced coo-min). Gently remove the plastic thing with the holes. Again, you are doing this because it'll take forever getting the clumps of cumin through the holes.
27. Throw out the plastic thing!
28. Gently shake out 2 teaspoons CUMIN into the measuring spoon.
29. Add CUMIN to the measuring cup. Screw on top.
30. When the oven timer goes off, add measuring cup CONTENTS to large pasta pot.
31. Set timer for 3 minutes. Keep stirring.
32. Place colander in sink.
33. Open 2 cans of BLACK BEANS. Pour BEANS into colander. Let them drain.
34. Open 1 can of STEWED TOMATOES.
35. Pour BEANS into saucepot over the sink, so not to spill. The saucepot is just a temporary holding place.

36. Rinse out colander.
37. Open 2 cans of BEER. Measure 1 Cup of BEER. Drink 1 can.
38. When oven timer goes off, slowly pour BEANS into large pasta pot.
39. Slowly pour ENTIRE CONTENTS OF TOMATO CAN into large pasta pot.
40. Slowly pour 1 Cup of BEER into large pasta pot. Stir CONTENTS.
41. Set oven timer for 15 minutes. Let everything simmer, which means, "bubble slightly, but not boil." (btw, I made that definition up.)
42. On cutting board, slice TOMATOES. Throw out both the tops and bottoms of TOMATOES.
43. Turn on WATER in sink. Take SLICED TOMATOES in your fingers and rinse off the icky, green SEEDS.
44. Drop clean TOMATOES into colander to dry.
45. Rinse colander.
46. Open SALAD BAG. Add SALAD to salad bowls.
47. When oven timer goes off, turn down FLAME to low.
48. Measure and add 10 ounces of CHEDDAR CHEESE to pasta pot.
49. Stir until CHEESE is melted and blended.
50. Once CHEESE is melted and blended, turn off flame.
51. Set oven timer for 5 minutes to let CHILI cool.
52. Add TOMATOES to salad bowls.
53. Grab BAG of MICROWAVABLE RICE. Open sides of top as instructed. Put BAG in microwave and cook for 90 seconds.
54. When RICE is done, remove bag and tear off top. Be careful, this mofo is hot! Let cool.
55. Add SALAD DRESSING to salads.
56. Pour remaining CHEDDAR CHEESE in bowl.
57. Carry SALADS and cheese bowl to table.
58. When oven timer goes off, spoon CHILI into bowls.
59. Pour RICE into serving bowl.
60. Carry CHILI and RICE to table.
61. Dinner is served!

Pransky's Turkey Picatta

This is Jen Pransky's second contribution to your culinary collection. (Check out her Dad's recipe for JERRY'S ROUND STEAK)

    Ease: 4 Chefs
    Cost: $50

Preparation Time: 15 minutes
Cooking Time: 15 minutes

Ingredients:
Turkey Breast Cutlets – 1.25 pounds; $5.99 *The cutlets should be no thicker than 1/8th of an inch. In other words: skinny. If they look too thick, place them between tin-foil and pound the shit out of them with your fists. This is a nice pre-date tension reliever.*
Sea Salt - ½ TEAspoon; $3.99
Cracked Black Pepper – ½ TEAspoon; $3.99
All-purpose Flour – 1/3 Cup; $3.00 per bag
Extra-Virgin Olive Oil – 2 TABLEspoons, divided; $6-13. (*"Divided" means you'll need it all but at different steps in the process*)
Dry White Wine – 1 Cup; $4 *THE WINE HAS TO BE DRY!*
Lemon – 1 sliced into 5 slices; 50 cents
Butter – 5 TABLEspoons "divided"; $5.50 for 4 sticks
Rice Pilaf – 1 Microwavable Bag; $2.49
Salad – 1 bag of pre-washed; $5
Tomatoes – 2; $2.99 per pound
Salad Dressing – Your Choice; $2
Take-n-Bake Bread – 1 loaf; $2.00 (*Found in Bakery section of supermarket*)

Recommended Wine: Chardonnay or, if feeling adventurous, Viognier

Tools, etc:
Cutting Board
Small Plate – 2
Large Plates – 3
Large Frying Pan – 1
Fork – 1
Measuring Cup – 1
Measuring Spoons
Stopwatch – 1
Serving Platter – 1
Large Salad Bowl – 1
Regular Salad Bowl – 2
Oven Mitt
Wooden Spoon
Serving Spoon

Directions:
1. 25 minutes before you want to eat, pre-heat oven.
2. Set oven timer for 5 minutes.
3. Wash LEMON in sink. Dry with paper towel.
4. On a cutting board, slice LEMON into 5 slices. Set aside on small plate #1 for later.
5. Cut 2 TABLEspoons of BUTTER and place them on lemon plate.

6. Remove rest of BUTTER from its wrapper. Place BUTTER on small plate #2 for later. This way it'll be nice and soft for bread by dinnertime.
7. When oven timer goes off, open TAKE-N-BAKE BREAD.
8. Put on oven mitt. Open oven door. Slide out rack.
9. Place BREAD on rack. Slide in rack. Close oven door. Take off oven mitt.
10. Set stopwatch for 15 minutes.
11. Take TURKEY CUTLETS out of package and put them on large plate #1.
12. Measure ½ TEAspoon of PEPPER in measuring spoon.
13. Use fingers to get a pinch of pepper. Then, sprinkle pepper all over – i.e. not just in a few spots – the CUTLETS.
14. Measure ½ TEAspoon of SALT in measuring spoon.
15. Use fingers to get a pinch of salt. Then, sprinkle salt all over the CUTLETS.
16. Measure 1/3 Cup of FLOUR. Pour FLOUR onto large plate #2.
17. Grab CUTLET and place it in FLOUR. Then, pick CUTLET up and do the same to the other side. Cutlet should be white on both sides.
18. Shake CUTLET to remove any excess flour. Place CUTLET on large plate #3.
19. Repeat steps 17 and 18 with all the remaining CUTLETS.
20. BEFORE YOU DO ANYTHING ELSE, wash off your fingers, which are now covered in a paper mache mixture of salt, pepper and flour.
21. Place frying pan on burner.
22. Measure 1 TABLEspoon of OLIVE OIL and pour into pan.
23. Turn on flame to highest heat. When OIL starts moving around very easily, you are ready for the cutlets.
24. Warning: Do NOT DROP CUTLETS into pan! SPLAT! OUCH!
25. Gently lay CUTLETS into the OIL.
26. Add as many CUTLETS to the frying pan as will fit comfortably (Don't wanna pack 'em in like, uh, veal).
27. Set oven timer for 1 minute. After 1 minute the cutlets will be golden brown.
28. Open BAG OF SALAD. Add to salad bowls.
29. When oven timer goes off, use fork to gently flip CUTLETS onto their other side.
30. Re-set oven timer for 1 minute.
31. Wash TOMATOES. Dry TOMATOES with paper towel. Place on counter.
32. When timer goes off, turn off flame.
33. Carry frying pan to serving platter.

34. Use fork to shake off excess OIL into frying pan. Place CUTLETS on serving platter.
35. When oven timer goes off, turn off oven.
36. Put on oven mitt. Open oven door. Slide out bottom rack.
37. Remove BREAD and place on cutting board.
38. Slide in rack. Close oven door. Take off oven mitt.
39. Time to cook the rest of the cutlets. You know how to do this, so show some swagger!
40. Return frying pan to burner.
41. Measure 1 TABLEspoon of OLIVE OIL and pour into frying pan.
42. Turn on flame to highest heat. When OIL starts moving around very easily, you are ready for the cutlets.
43. Remember: Gently lay CUTLETS into the OIL.
44. Add remaining CUTLETS to the frying pan.
45. Set oven timer for 1 minute. After 1 minute the cutlets will be golden brown.
46. Slice ¼ Loaf of BREAD. Put 2 SLICES on each dinner plate.
47. When oven timer goes off, use fork to gently flip CUTLETS onto their other side.
48. Re-set timer for 1 minute.
49. Place colander in sink.
50. When timer goes off, turn off flame.
51. Carry frying pan to serving platter.
52. Use fork to shake off excess OIL and then place CUTLETS on serving platter. Don't stack them like pancakes; arrange them around the edges first, then in center.
53. Return frying pan to stovetop burner.
54. Slice TOMATOES on cutting board. Throw out both the tops and bottoms of TOMATOES.
55. Turn on WATER in sink. Take SLICED TOMATOES in your fingers and rinse the icky, green SEEDS off. Drop clean TOMATOES into colander.
56. Carefully move flour plate to counter next to sink. (Seriously, this is a major disaster just waiting to happen, so get the plate there neatly.)
57. Place equal amounts of SLICED TOMATOES in each salad bowl.
58. Place flour plate in sink. Run WATER to prevent any future dust cloud.
59. Now, back to the frying pan. DO NOT TURN ON FLAME YET!!!!
60. Measure 1 Cup of DRY WHITE WINE and add to frying pan.
61. Add LEMON SLICES to frying pan.
62. Turn on flame to highest heat. Once MIXTURE starts to boil, use wooden spoon to scrape up yummy, browned stuff at the bottom.

63. Add 2 TABLEspoons of BUTTER to frying pan.
64. Use wooden spoon to swirl BUTTER until it melts.
65. When BUTTER has melted, turn off the flame under frying pan.
66. Carefully carry frying pan to the serving platter.
67. Pour the MIXTURE all over the CUTLETS. Be sure LEMON SLICES are on top of CUTLETS.
68. Return frying pan to stovetop burner.
69. Open top of MICROWAVABLE RICE BAG as instructed on packet. Place in microwave and cook for 90 seconds.
70. Add SALAD DRESSING to SALAD.
71. Carry salad bowls and butter plate to table.
72. When RICE is done, carefully open BAG (seriously, this mofo is hot!).
73. Pour half the RICE on one plate, and the remaining half on the other.
74. Carry dinner plates to table.
75. Add serving spoon to serving plate (for scooping sauce onto cutlets).
76. Carry serving plate to table.
77. Dinner is served!

PORK

Ammo's Honey-Mustard Pork Chops

I'm ten years older than my sister, Anne-Marie, so when I moved out of the house she was not yet working magic in the kitchen. I missed out!

Ease: 1 Chef
Cost: $33.50
Preparation Time: 5 minutes
Cooking Time: 45 minutes

Ingredients:
Pork Chops – 4; $8.50 per package
Boar's Head Honey Mustard – 6 TABLEspoons; $2.99 *(You have to get a high-end honey-mustard, NOT the generic kind because my sister insisted on making you combine real honey with mustard and I decided that was simply cruel and inhuman treatment)*
Bread Crumbs – 1 Cup; $1.79
Wild Rice – 1 Microwavable Bag; $2.49
Salad – 1 Bag pre-washed; $5
Tomatoes – 2; $2.99 per pound
Salad Dressing – Bottle of your choice; $2
Take-n-Bake Bread – 1 Loaf; $2.00 *(Found in Bakery section of supermarket)*
Butter – 4 TABLEspoons; $5.50 per 4 sticks

Wine Recommendation: Cabernet or, if feeling adventurous, Australian Grenache (pronounced gren-ash)

Tools, etc:
Large Baking Pan
Paper Towels
Measuring Spoons
Large Plate
Shallow Bowl
Fork
Colander (the thingy with all the holes; it's for draining things)
Paring Knife
Thin Spatula
Instant-Read Meat Thermometer

Directions:
1. Pre-heat oven to 350 degrees.
2. Spray large baking pan with NON-STICK SPRAY.
3. Wash PORK CHOPS under cold water in sink. Dry CHOPS with paper towels.
4. Wash HANDS. Then, wash faucet knob afterwards because it'll be GROSS from your fingers getting slimy after handling the pork chops.
5. Measure 6 TABLEspoons of HONEY MUSTARD and add to large plate.
6. Measure 1 Cup of BREAD CRUMBS and add to shallow bowl.
7. Pick up 1 PORK CHOP and place it in the middle of the MUSTARD on the large plate. Push down on the CHOP to make sure it gets all mustardy.
8. With a fork, pick up PORK CHOP and flip it onto its other side. Again, push down on it.
9. Use fork to scoop up extra MUSTARD and cover any bare parts of PORK.
10. With a fork, pick up PORK CHOP and gently place it in the BREADCRUMBS. Seriously, the CRUMBS will leap the banks of the bowl if you go too hard.
11. With a fork, pick up PORK CHOP and flip it onto its other side.
12. Move PORK CHOP to large baking pan.
13. Repeat steps 7 – 12 with the remaining 3 PORK CHOPS.
14. Put on oven mitt. Open oven door. Slide out rack.
15. Place large baking dish on rack. Slide in rack. Close oven door.
16. Set oven timer for 35 minutes. Take off oven mitt.
17. Wash TOMATOES. Pat dry with paper towels.
18. Cut 4 TABLEspoons of BUTTER (Use the ruler on the wax paper wrapper to measure this) and put BUTTER on small plate for later.
19. Put colander in sink.
20. Open BAG OF SALAD. Add SALAD to salad bowls.
21. On the cutting board, chop TOMATOES. Throw out TOPS and BOTTOMS of TOMATOES.
22. Run WATER in sink. Rinse off icky, green SEEDS from TOMATOES. Then, drop TOMATOES into colander to dry.
23. When oven timer goes off, open TAKE-N-BAKE BREAD.
24. Put on oven mitt. Open oven door. Slide out bottom rack.
25. Place BREAD on bottom rack. Slide in rack. Close oven door.
26. Re-set oven timer for 10 minutes. Take off oven mitt.
27. Add TOMATOES to salad bowls.
28. When oven timer goes off, put on oven mitt. Open oven door. Slide out rack with PORK CHOPS.

29. Place large baking pan on stovetop burners.
30. Slide in rack. Close oven door.
31. Stick instant-read meat thermometer into a CHOP. The temperature must be 155 degrees or Ms. Right Now might die.
32. If the temperature is 155 or higher, the PORK is done. But if the temperature is lower than 155, return the baking dish back to the oven for 5 minutes.
33. Once the PORK is done, re-set oven timer for 5 minutes. Turn up oven's heat to 500 degrees.
34. Add SALAD DRESSING to SALADS.
35. Rip top of BAG OF RICE according to directions. Cook in microwave for 90 seconds.
36. Carry butter plate and salad bowls to table.
37. When RICE is done, remove bag and tear off top. Be careful, this mofo is hot!
38. Pour half the RICE onto each dinner plate.
39. With the thin spatula (this lets you keep most of the mustardy bread crumbs on the bottom) place 1 PORK CHOP on each dinner plate.
40. When timer goes off, turn off oven.
41. Put on oven mitt. Open oven door. Slide out bottom rack.
42. Remove BREAD and place on cutting board.
43. Slide in rack. Close oven door. Take off oven mitt.
44. Slice ¼ Loaf of BREAD. Put 2 SLICES on each dinner plate.
45. Carry dinner plates to table.
46. Dinner is served!

Steve's "Easy P ork" Tenderloin

Steve Egan gleefully intended the double entendre in the title.

In 1997, two friends and I paid Steve a total of $15 to drink the warm "bricks" left over from our keg party the night before. Merely typing that sentence caused me to dry heave again. And here I am, asking for and taking his culinary advice.

The owner of South Bend, Indiana's first cool coffee bar, Lula's Café, Steve liked to cook real meals long before any other straight guy I know. It must have worked, since his college girlfriend never gave him the chance to sample the single life. (You can check out Michelle's family's dynamite recipe for potatoes in the "Sides" section. Look for "Poeppe's Potatoes.")

Ease: 2 Chefs
Cost: $53
Preparation Time: 15 minutes
Cooking Time: 25 minutes per pound; so, approximately, 100 minutes total

Ingredients:
Center Cut Pork Tenderloin – 4 pounds; $6.99 per 20-ounce package (*Do not freeze it after you buy it; just store it in the fridge*)
Extra Virgin Olive Oil – 8 TABLEspoons; $6-13 per bottle
Balsamic Vinegar – 8 TABLEspoons; $2-8 per bottle
Honey Dijon Mustard – 4 TABLEspoons; $3.00
Garlic Salt – 1 TABLEspoon; $2.99 per jar
Butter – 4 TABLEspoons; $5.50 per 4-sticks
Bag of Pre-washed Salad; $5.00
Tomatoes – 4; $2.99 per pound
Salad Dressing – 1 bottle of your choice; 2.00
Take-n-Bake Bread – 1 loaf; $2.00 (*Found in Bakery section of supermarket*)

Recommended Wine: Pinot Noir or, if feeling adventurous, Bordeaux

Tools, etc:
Measuring Spoons
Mixing Bowl
Large Baking Dish
Paring Knife
Basting Brush
Oven Mitts – 2
Paper Towels
Colander
Cutting Board
Meat Thermometer
Tinfoil
Bowls – 2
Dinner Spoon
Instant-Read Meat Thermometer

Directions:

1. Preheat oven to 350 degrees.

2. Measure 8 TABLEspoons of OLIVE OIL and add to mixing bowl.

3. Measure 8 TABLEspoons of BALSAMIC VINEGAR and add to mixing bowl.

4. Measure 4 TABLEspoons of HONEY-DIJON MUSTARD and add to mixing bowl.

5. Stir mixing bowl CONTENTS until one consistent liquid.

6. Measure 1 TABLEspoon of GARLIC SALT and sprinkle on the bottom of large baking dish. (This wasn't in Steve's recipe, but I'm crazy like that. And since the meal turned out great, you probably don't want to jinx it.)

7. Place TENDERLOIN in baking dish.

8. Use paring knife to slice thin cuts on top of each rib. This will help the sauce soak into the meat.

9. Use basting brush to cover the TENDERLOIN with half the SAUCE. (You will use the remaining half later.)
10. Put on oven mitt. Open oven door. Slide out oven rack. Place baking dish on oven rack. Close oven door.
11. Set oven timer for 50 minutes. Take off oven mitt.
12. Put colander in the sink.
13. Wash TOMATOES in sink. Dry TOMATOES with paper towel.
14. Open BAG OF SALAD and add to salad bowls.
15. On cutting board, chop TOMATOES. Use faucet to rinse off GOOEY, GREEN SEEDS.
16. Place CHOPPED TOMATOES in colander to dry.
17. When timer goes off, put on oven mitt. Open oven door. Slide out rack.
18. Pull out baking dish and place it on stovetop burners.
19. Slide in rack. Close oven door. Take off oven mitt.
20. Use basting brush to re-coat TENDERLOIN with second half of SAUCE still in mixing bowl. Pour any remaining SAUCE all over the meat.
21. Put on oven mitt. Open oven door. Slide out rack. Place baking dish on rack. Slide in rack. Close oven door.
22. Set oven timer for 50 minutes. Take off oven mitt.
23. Measure 4 TABLEspoons of BUTTER (Use the ruler on the wax paper wrapper to do this) and add to a small plate.
24. When oven timer goes off, put on oven mitt.
25. Open door. Slide out rack. Place baking dish on burners again. Slide in rack. Close door.
26. Grab meat thermometer and check the meat's temperature.
27. If temperature is below 155 degrees, put the baking dish back in the oven for 5 minutes.
28. If temperature is 155 degrees or higher, keep baking dish on stovetop burners.
29. With the baking dish on the burners, you will "tent" the TENDERLOIN.
30. Tear off a sheet of tinfoil and place it over the MEAT. Do not cover it tightly; simply lay the infoil on top of the meat like a blanket.
31. Open TAKE-N-BAKE BREAD.
32. Put on oven mitt. Open oven door. Slide out bottom rack.
33. Place BREAD on bottom rack. Slide in rack. Close oven door. Take off oven mitt.
34. Increase oven to 400 degrees.
35. Set the oven timer for 10 minutes.
36. Add TOMATOES to salad bowls.

37. When oven timer goes off, remove tinfoil from TENDERLOIN.
38. Re-set oven timer for 5 minutes.
39. Slightly open top of bag of RICE as instructed.
40. Place RICE in microwave. Cook for 90 seconds.
41. Slice PORK LOINS and place 2 LOINS on each dinner plate.
42. When RICE is done, carefully open top of bag to allow steam to escape. Watch out; this mofo is really freaking hot!
43. Pour half the RICE onto each dinner plate.
44. Move TENDERLOIN to a spare plate. Put on two oven mitts.
45. Lift baking dish and carefully pour JUICES into last clean bowl.
46. Return TENDERLOIN to baking dish. Take off oven mitts.
47. Add SALAD DRESSING to salads.
48. Carry SALADS and butter plate out to the table.
49. Carry dinner plates and sauce bowl out to the table.
50. Dinner is served!

SEAFOOD

Suzy's Baked Salmon

As a Colonel in the U.S. Army's J.A.G. Corps, Suzy Mitchem can bring home the bacon, fry it up in the pan…and fry your ass if you're late for dinner.

This recipe requires two uses of the oven: baking and broiling.

The broiler is located in the lower part of the oven, that small, seemingly useless door underneath the big one where you cook frozen pizza. Unlike a barbeque grill where the flame is below the food, a broiler works with the flame *above* the food.

The broiler affords the cook flexibility in terms of proximity to the flame. Most broilers have two settings: HI and LOW, i.e. close to the flame and further from it.

Let me start by saying I have always been terrified of the broiler; never used it and wasn't willing to try. But after finally popping my cherry in order to write this book, I am now kicking myself for ignoring this convenient tool. What a breeze!

You have to wash the broiler pan prior to using it, though, since it likely hasn't been washed since you moved into your place.

Ease: 1 Chef
Cost: $37
Preparation Time: 5 minutes
Cooking Time: 17 minutes

Ingredients:
Salmon – 2 eight-ounce Filets; $5.99 per pound
Dijon Mustard – 2 TABLEspoons "divided"; $1.99 per jar ("Divided" means split up to be used separately)
Cajun Seasonings – ½ TEAspoon divided; $6.29 per bottle
Tarragon – ¼ TEAspoon; $7.19 per bottle
Yellow Rice – 1 Microwavable Bag; $2.49
Pre-Washed Salad – 1 bag; $5.00
Tomatoes – 4; $2.99
Salad Dressing – 1 bottle of your choice; $2.00
Italian Bread – 1 Loaf; $2.29

Recommended Wine: Zinfandel or, if feeling adventurous, Tempranillo

Tools, etc:
Baking Dish
Tin Foil
Measuring Spoons
Knife
Cutting Board

Spatula
Oven Mitt
Colander (Plastic thingy with the holes in it)

Directions:
1. Open broiler door and remove broiler pan. This is what you're going to cook the salmon on.
2. Rinse off the broiler pan and dry it with paper towels. Return boiler pan and shut broiler door.
3. Pre-heat oven to 450.
4. Wash off SALMON FILETS in sink. Pat dry with paper towels.
5. Line baking dish with tin foil.
6. Place SALMON skin-side down in baking dish.
7. Measure 1 TABLEspoon of DIJON MUSTARD.
8. Spread and cover the whole FILET #1. (Note: A lot of MUSTARD will remain stuck inside spoon; use your finger to get it out and then add it to the FILET.) If 1 TABLEspoon isn't enough, just use as much mustard as you need to cover the whole FILET.
9. Repeat Step 8 for FILET #2.
10. Measure ¼ TEAspoon of CAJUN SEASONINGS. Sprinkle all over the MUSTARD on FILET #1. Repeat for FILET #2.
11. Carefully open the TARRAON BOTTLE. Seriously, they will spray all over!
12. Hold out your left palm. Shake the BOTTLE twice into your palm.
13. Use your fingers to take a pinch of TARRAGON LEAVES. Sprinkle on top of the CAJUN SEASONINGS on FILET #1.
14. Take another pinch of TARRAGON. Sprinkle on FILET #2.
15. Put on oven mitt. Open oven door and slide out rack.
16. Place baking dish on rack. Slide in rack. Close door.
17. Set oven timer for 13 minutes. Take off oven mitt.
18. Cut 4 TABLEspoons of BUTTER (Use the ruler on the wax paper wrapper to measure this) and put BUTTER on small plate for later.
19. On cutting board, slice ¼ of ITALIAN BREAD.
20. Place 2 slices on each dinner plate.
21. Place colander in sink.
22. Wash TOMATOES. Dry TOMATOES with paper towel.
23. On cutting board, slice TOMATOES. Throw out both the tops and bottoms of TOMATOES.
24. Turn on WATER in sink. Take SLICED TOMATOES in your fingers and rinse off the icky, green SEEDS.

25. Drop clean TOMATOES into colander to dry.
26. When oven timer goes off, put on oven mitt.
27. Open oven door and slide out rack.
28. Take baking dish and place it perpendicularly on unlit stovetop burners.
29. Slide in rack. Close door.
30. Open broiler door. Take out broiler pan.
31. Place boiler pan perpendicularly on stovetop burners next to baking dish.
32. Spray broiler pan with NON-STICK SPRAY.
33. Use spatula to move FILETS from baking dish to broiler pan.
34. Take broiler pan and place in broiler on HIGH SETTING.
35. Close broiler door. Take off oven mitt.
36. Re-set oven timer for 5 minutes. This will make the top of the salmon crispy.
37. Open BAG OF SALAD. Add to two salad bowls.
38. Check SALMON to make sure it's not burning!
39. Add equal amounts of SLICED TOMATOES to salad bowls.
40. Check SALMON again to make sure it's still not burning!
41. When oven timer goes off, turn off broiler.
42. Put on oven mitt. Open broiler door and slide out rack.
43. Remove broiler pan and place it onto unlit burners.
44. Slide in rack. Close door. Take off oven mitt.
45. Allow SALMON to cool for a bit.
46. Add SALAD DRESSING to SALADS.
47. Grab BAG of MICROWAVABLE RICE. Open top's sides as instructed.
48. Put BAG in microwave and cook for 90 seconds.
49. Carry salad bowls and butter plate to table.
50. When RICE is done, remove bag and carefully tear off top. Careful; hot!
51. Place 1 SALMON FILET on each dinner plate.
52. Pour ½ bag of RICE onto each dinner plate.
53. Carry dinner plates to table.
54. Dinner is served!

Chef Zach's Lemon-Caper Swordfish & Arugula Salad

Zach McGowan has cooked on the Food Network show "2 Dudes Catering". He says this flavor combination is one of his favorites.
It will soon be one of yours, too. (Check out his LASAGNA BOLOGNESE.)

Ease: 2 Chefs
Cost: $54
Preparation Time: 20 minutes
Cooking Time: 8 minutes

Ingredients:
Swordfish – 2 eight-ounce steaks; $6.00 per steak
Arugula Salad – 1 Bag pre-washed; $4.29
Extra Virgin Olive Oil – 2 TABLEspoons; $6-13 per bottle
Non-Pareil Capers – 2 TABLEspoons; $4.39 per jar. (*Capers can be found in the Pickle aisle of the grocery store. Make sure the capers are the "non-pareil" kind*)
Red Onion – 1; $.85
Lemons – 2; $1.00 each
Shredded Parmesan Cheese – 1.5 Cups; $3.99 per 16-ounce bag
White Balsamic Vinegar – 1 TABLEspoon; $4.29 per bottle
Sea Salt – ¼ TEAspoon; $1.34 per shaker
Yellow Rice – 1 Microwavable Bag; $2.49
Italian Bread – 1 Loaf; $2.29
Butter – 6 TABLEspoons "divided"; $5.50 per package (*"Divided" means the ingredients will be used at different steps of the process*)

Wine Recommendation: Sauvignon Blanc or, if feeling adventurous, Viognier

Tools, etc:
Large Serving Bowl
Cutting Board
Chopping Knife
Large Plate
Measuring Spoons
Stopwatch
Metal Frying Pan
Small Plate – 2
Oven Mitts
Wooden Spoon
Colander (the thingy with all the holes; it's for draining pasta)

Directions:
1. Open ARUGULA BAG and empty SALAD into large serving bowl.
2. If you don't want to cry while chopping ONIONS, take a dinner spoon and suck on it. Seriously.
3. On cutting board, chop off both ends of the RED ONION.

4. Cut the REMAINDER in half.
5. Remove ONION SKIN and throw the skin in the trash.
6. You now have a halved red onion that has been cut on two sides.
7. Turn ONION so that 1 cut side faces you. Choose 1 UNCUT SIDE.
8. Thinly slice along that uncut side. Place ONION in measuring cup. You want ½ Cup of sliced onions. The point here is to slice the onion as thinly as possible. Think of it like a wet t-shirt contest, only instead of "Skin to Win!" this motto is, "Thin to Win!"
9. Use your fingers to evenly spread out the ONION in the large serving bowl.
10. Furiously scrub hands with DISH SOAP. ONION will stink up your cuticles, which won't go over well later when you try to feed her dessert.
11. Measure 1.5 Cups of PARMESAN CHEESE. Add CHEESE to large serving bowl.
12. Put large serving bowl in fridge, as you won't need it for a while.
13. Cover large plate with paper towels. This will help you dry up any moisture on the steaks.
14. Unwrap SWORDFISH. Throw out plastic and butcher paper. You'll want to take out the trash way before she gets there!
15. Place SWORDFISH on top of paper towels on plate. Push down on SWORDFISH so the paper towels soak up moisture on bottom.
16. Take another paper towel and soak up moisture on top of the STEAKS.
17. Throw out all paper towels.
18. Place frying pan on burner. Crank up HEAT. Turn on oven vent fan.
19. Measure ¼ TEAspoon of OLIVE OIL and pour on 1 STEAK.
20. Repeat step 19 for second STEAK.
21. Use your fingers to rub the OLIVE OIL onto every millimeter of fish.
22. Use fork to flip STEAKS.
23. Repeat step 21 for each STEAK.
24. Wash hands.
25. Measure ¼ TEAspoon of SEA SALT. Use fingers to take pinch.
26. Sprinkle SALT all over STEAK. Then, sprinkle another pinch on the other STEAK.
27. Use fork to flip STEAKS.
28. Repeat steps 25-26 for each STEAK.
29. By now the frying pan is hot enough. Use fork to place STEAKS in pan. (The oil that's already on the fish will keep it from sticking to the pan.)
30. Set oven timer for 5 minutes.
31. Once the STEAKS are in the pan, DO NOT TOUCH THEM until it is time to flip them!

32. Slice ¼ loaf of ITALIAN BREAD and add to dinner plates.
33. Slice a LEMON in half and leave them on a plate.
34. Slice 2 TABLEspoons of BUTTER (Use the ruler on the wax paper wrapper to measure this) and leave them on the lemon plate. Move the plate close to the frying pan.
35. Slice 4 TABLEspoons of BUTTER and place on a small plate for later.
36. Place colander in sink. Grab CAPERS.
37. Do the next move over the colander.
38. Measure 1 TABLEspoon of CAPERS and pour it into the colander. (We don't want the capers juice, just the capers)
39. Measure another TABLEspoon of CAPERS and pour it into the colander.
40. When the oven timer goes off, flip STEAKS.
41. Re-set oven timer for 2 minutes and 30 seconds.
42. When the oven timer goes off, remove STEAKS and place on a plate. Keep flame on underneath pan!
43. Throw 2 Tablespoons of BUTTER into the pan.
44. When BUTTER melts, pour CAPERS into pan.
45. Squeeze 2 LEMON HALVES into frying pan.
46. Turn off flame. Move frying pan to a cool burner.
47. Stir MIXTURE in frying pan.
48. Remove salad bowl from fridge.
49. Measure 1 TABLEspoon of OLIVE OIL and pour all over SALAD.
50. Measure 1 TABLEspoon of WHITE BALSAMIC VINEGAR and pour over SALAD.
51. Measure ¼ TEAspoon of SEA SALT. Take a pinch and sprinkle it all over the SALAD.
52. Grab BAG of MICROWAVABLE RICE. Open sides of top as instructed.
53. Put RICE BAG in microwave and cook for 90 seconds.
54. Toss SALAD.
55. Carry butter plate to table.
56. When RICE is done, remove bag and carefully tear off top. Watch out; this mofo is hot!
57. Position two dinner plates on the counter.
58. Grab 2 handfuls of SALAD and cover ¾ of the plate. Repeat with the other plate.
59. Pour half the RICE onto one plate and half on the other plate.
60. Place each STEAK so that half the STEAK sits on the SALAD and half on the plate.
61. Grab the frying pan and the wooden spoon.

62. Spoon the LEMON CAPER SAUCE onto the STEAKS. Make sure each STEAK has plenty of CAPERS!

63. Carry dinner plates to table.

64. Dinner is served!

Johanna's Basil Shrimp

Johanna Vaughan-Chen is a ballet instructor and an artist and a damn fine cook. She landed my friend Ranah with meals like this! (Maybe her long legs helped.) She describes her shrimp pasta as an "easy-for-a-guy-to-make-but-foolproof-to-impress-the-chick" recipe. It's the most aesthetically pleasing meal in *Bachelor 101*.

Johanna's original recipe is a bit fancier, but this version is EASIER.

Ease: 3 Chefs. *This is like a black diamond ski run that you accidentally find yourself on, but then it turns out to have been groomed and when you get to the bottom you laugh at how scared you had been before you started down.*

Cost: $73

Preparation Time: 3 hours. *Don't have a heart attack. You need to marinate the shrimp for at least 3 hours prior to grilling. The longer the shrimp soak in the marinade, the better.*

Cooking Time: 40 minutes. 99% of which is boiling the water for the pasta and then cooking the pasta. The shrimp only take 1 minute, 30 seconds for each side.

Ingredients:
Jumbo Shrimp – 20 cooked, peeled and de-veined; $18.00 per pound (You want the kind that you'd see in a restaurant's shrimp cocktail)
Farfalle (a.k.a. "Bowtie" Pasta) – 1 sixteen-ounce Box; $2.79
Shredded Mozzarella Cheese – 1 sixteen-ounce Bag; $4.99
Cherry Tomatoes – 20; $3.99 *These are sometimes called "Grape" or "Sweet" tomatoes. There might be slight differences between them all, but for our purposes they are the same damn thing – a tiny tomato.*
Fresh Basil – no exact amount; $1.99
Dried Basil Flakes – no exact amount; $4.39
Olive Oil – 11 TABLEspoons "divided"; $6-13 per bottle. *"Divided" means it will be used at different steps in the process.*
Cayenne Pepper – no exact amount; $6.29
Garlic Powder – no exact amount; $4.69
Sea Salt – no exact amount; $3.99
Cracked Black Pepper – no exact amount; $3.99
Bag of Pre-washed Salad; $5.00
Salad Dressing – 1 bottle of your choice; $2.00
Take-n-Bake Bread – 1 Loaf; $2.00 (*Found in Bakery section of supermarket*)

Wine Recommendation: Chardonnay or, if feeling adventurous, Dolcetto

Tools, etc:
Large Ziploc Bag - 1

Measuring Spoons
Small Plate – 2
Pasta Pot - Large
Colander (the thingy with all the holes; it's for draining stuff in the sink)
Pretty Bowl – Large. *If you now find yourself saying, "Pretty bird, pretty bird" over and over like the blind kid in "Dumb and Dumber," that's normal.*
Cutting Board
Stopwatch
Paring Knife
Wooden Spoon
Tongs
Tinfoil

Directions:

1. Wash off SHRIMP in sink. Pat dry with paper towels.
2. Measure 4 TABLEspoons of OLIVE OIL and add to Ziploc bag.
3. Add 5 shakes of SALT and 5 cranks of PEPPER (Johanna used the verb "twirls", but that's masculine enough for us) to the Ziploc bag.
4. Add 5 shakes of CAYENNE PEPPER to the Ziploc bag.
5. Add 2 shakes of GARLIC POWDER to the Ziploc bag.
6. Add 3 shakes of BASIL FLAKES to the Ziploc bag.
7. Place SHRIMP in Ziploc bag.
8. Seal Ziploc bag. Shake bag like crazy for 45 seconds, to cover shrimp with marinade.
9. Place bag in fridge for 3 hours. Make sure the SHRIMP are soaking in marinade at the bottom of the bag.
10. Slice 4 TABLEspoons of BUTTER (Use the ruler on the wax paper wrapper to measure) and place on small plate #1 for later with dinner.
11. 30 minutes before you want to eat, fill large pasta pot with amount of WATER recommended in PASTA directions.
12. Put large pasta pot on stovetop burner and cover.
13. Turn on flame to high heat.
14. Place colander in sink.
15. WASH TOMATOES above colander and let them dry in the colander.
16. 20 minutes before you want to eat, preheat oven to 400 degrees.
17. Set oven timer for 5 minutes.
18. When oven timer goes off, open TAKE-N-BAKE BREAD.
19. Put on oven mitt. Open oven door. Slide out rack.
20. Place BREAD on rack.

21. Slide in rack. Close oven door. Take off oven mitt.
22. Set oven timer for 15 minutes.
23. Take out large serving bowl.
24. Measure 5 TABLEspoons of OLIVE OIL and add to large serving bowl.
25. Chop up or rip apart (you'll feel manlier) ½ package of FRESH BASIL LEAVES. Add CHOPPED/RIPPED BASIL to large serving bowl.
26. Put cutting board next to colander in sink.
27. Put 2 TOMATOES onto cutting board. This is gonna get super messy, with the tomatoes' green guts exploding all over the place; ergo, cutting them in the sink.
28. Take paring knife and slice TOMATOES in half.
29. Turn on WATER and rinse out any remaining ICKY GREEN SEEDS.
30. Add TOMATOES to large serving bowl.
31. Repeat steps 25-28 for all the TOMATOES.
32. Rinse out colander. Leave colander in sink.
33. Open BAG of MOZZARELLA and dump all into large serving bowl.
34. Add 6 shakes of SEA SALT to large pretty bowl.
35. Add 10 cranks of CRACKED PEPPER to large pretty bowl.
36. Use wooden spoon to gently stir MIXTURE. Leave large serving bowl on counter at room temperature.
37. When the WATER boils, add 6 shakes of SEA SALT to pasta pot.
38. Add PASTA and stir.
39. Set stopwatch for the amount of time on the PASTA BOX directions.
40. Open BAG OF SALAD and add to salad bowls.
41. Place large frying pan on a stovetop burner.
42. When the stopwatch goes off, turn off flame under pasta pot.
43. Put on oven mitt and carry pasta pot to sink.
44. Pour PASTA and WATER into colander. Shake colander.
45. Place large serving bowl next to sink.
46. Take off oven mitt.
47. As soon as the PASTA is done draining, quickly grab the colander and dump the pasta into the large serving bowl. (Speed is important here to keep the pasta very hot.)
48. Using the wooden spoon, mix the contents thoroughly but gently.
49. Immediately cover the serving bowl with tinfoil. The piping hot pasta will melt the cheese and cook tomatoes lightly.

50. When oven timer goes off, turn off oven.
51. Put on oven mitt. Open oven door. Slide out bottom rack.
52. Remove BREAD and place on cutting board.
53. Slide in rack. Close oven door. Take off oven mitt.
54. Turn on flame under frying pan to high heat.
55. Get SHRIMP Ziploc bag out of fridge.
56. Measure 2 TABLEspoons of OLIVE OIL and add to frying pan.
57. Measure 2 TABLEspoons of BUTTER (Use the ruler on the wax paper to do this) and add to the frying pan.
58. Don't let BUTTER in frying pan boil!
59. As soon as BUTTER melts, add the SHRIMP to the frying pan.
60. Set oven timer for 30 seconds. This is the advantage of buying pre-cooked shrimp – you don't have to worry whether you cooked them enough, etc!
61. Make sure SHRIMP all make contact with bottom of frying pan.
62. Throw out Ziploc bag.
63. When oven timer goes off, use tongs to flip SHRIMP.
64. Re-set timer for 30 seconds.
65. When timer goes off, turn off flame.
66. Place dinner plates on counter.
67. Use tongs to place half the SHRIMP around the outside of one plate, then the other plate.
68. Slice ¼ Loaf of BREAD. Put 2 SLICES on each dinner plate.
69. Add SALAD DRESSING to salads.
70. Carry butter plate and bread plate to the table.
71. Carry salad bowls to the table.
72. Carry shrimp plates out to the table.
73. Uncover large serving bowl and carry it to the table.
74. Spoon Ms. Right Now's PASTA into the empty space on her dinner plate, then serve your own.
75. Dinner is served!

Brent's Shrimp Scampi

If not for his being a Red Sox fan, Brent Pickett might be considered the perfect man.
    He taught skiing in Europe, made Teak furniture by hand and married a cute pediatrician who swam at Stanford. I am pretty sure I hate him. (Check out Brent's Veggie Pasta.)

When Brent first suggested Shrimp Scampi, I assumed he lacked a working definition of "easy recipe." This meal requires <u>sautéing</u> the shrimp.

Sounds scary, right? I thought so, too. Then I learned "sauté" means "To fry quickly in a little fat." Put even more simply, sauté means you get a frying pan really hot, toss in some butter or olive oil and then add the ingredients. Voila.

Thanks, Brent, for making me less of an ignoramus.

Ease: 3 Chefs
Cost: $59
Preparation Time: 10 minutes
Cooking Time: 20 minutes (including boiling water for pasta)

Ingredients:
Jumbo Shrimp – 20 peeled, de-veined and cooked; $18.00 per pound (You want the kind that you'd see in a restaurant's shrimp cocktail)
Angel Hair Pasta – 1 pound; $2.55 per 16-ounce box
Extra Virgin Olive Oil – 3 TABLEspoons "divided"; $6-13 per bottle ("Divided" Means "split up to be used separately")
Minced Garlic – 2 TEAspoons; $1.99-6.99 per jar
Sea Salt – 1 TEAspoon; $1.19 per shaker
Butter – 2 TABLEspoons; $5.50 per package of 4 sticks
Oregano – 1 TEAspoon; $4.99
Shredded Parmesan Cheese – 1 sixteen-ounce Bag; $3.99
Pre-Washed Salad – 1 bag; $5.00
Tomatoes – 4; $2.99
Salad Dressing – 1 bottle of your choice; $2.00
Take-n-Bake Bread – 1 Loaf; $2.00 (*Found in Bakery section of supermarket*)

Recommended Wine: Sauvignon Blanc or, if feeling adventurous, Riesling

Tools, etc:
Gallon sized Ziploc Bag – 1
Large Pasta Pot
Measuring Spoons
Large Frying Pan
Wooden Spoon
Colander (Plastic thingy with the holes in it)
Large Serving Bowl
Tongs

Directions:

1. Place STICK of BUTTER on counter.

2. Fill pasta pot with amount of WATER required in ANGEL HAIR instructions.

3. Cover pasta pot and crank up flame to high.

4. Wash off SHRIMP in sink. Pat dry with paper towels.

5. Measure 1 TABLEspoon of OLIVE OIL. Pour OLIVE OIL into Ziploc bag.

6. Measure 2 TEAspoons of MINCED GARLIC. "Pour" GARLIC into Ziploc bag. Pouring isn't the correct term for this technique, as the GARLIC will not emerge so willingly. Use your finger to get out garlic that remains in the measuring spoon and then add the garlic to the Ziploc bag.
7. Add SHRIMP to Ziploc bag. Seal bag. Grasping top of the bag, shake bag for 10 seconds. All the SHRIMP should now be covered with garlic and oil.
8. Place Ziploc bag on counter.
9. When the WATER boils, add ANGEL HAIR PASTA to pasta pot.
10. Measure 1 TEAspoon of SEA SALT. Add SALT to pasta pot. Stir.
11. Set timer for amount of time specified on ANGEL HAIR BOX.
12. Put large frying pan on burner. Do not turn on flame.
13. Open BAG OF SALAD. Add to two salad bowls.
14. Wash TOMATOES. Dry TOMATOES with paper towel.
15. Place colander in sink.
16. On cutting board, slice TOMATOES. Throw out both the tops and bottoms of TOMATOES.
17. Turn on WATER in sink. Take SLICED TOMATOES in your fingers and rinse off the icky, green SEEDS. Then, drop clean TOMATOES into colander to dry.
18. Slice a quarter of the ITALIAN BREAD.
19. Add equal amounts of SLICED TOMATOES to salad bowls.
20. Rinse out colander.
21. When oven timer goes off, turn off flame under pasta pot.
22. Carefully carry pasta pot to sink and pour PASTA into colander to drain.
23. Men, it's time to sautee the SHRIMP.
24. Turn on flame under frying pan to high heat. Count to 15.
25. Measure 2 TABLEspoons of OLIVE OIL. Pour OLIVE OIL into frying pan.
26. Slice 2 TABLEspoons of BUTTER. Add BUTTER to frying pan.
27. Move remainder of BUTTER from wrapper to small plate for later.
28. Don't let BUTTER boil in frying pan! As soon as BUTTER melts, add the SHRIMP/GARLIC/OIL MIXTURE to the frying pan.
29. Set timer for 30 seconds. This is an advantage of buying pre-cooked shrimp – you don't have to worry whether you cooked them enough, etc. You just have to warm them up a bit!
30. Make sure SHRIMP all make contact with frying pan.
31. When timer goes off, flip SHRIMP. Re-set timer for 30 seconds.
32. Measure 1 TEAspoon of OREGANO. Sprinkle OREGANO all over frying pan. Stir OREGANO in.

33. When oven timer goes off, turn off flame.
34. Pour PASTA into large serving bowl.
35. Carefully pour SHRIMP MIXTURE over PASTA. Grab wooden spoon and scrape every drop of SAUCE onto pasta.
36. Add SALAD DRESSING to SALAD.
37. Carry salad bowls and butter plate to table.
38. Place one slice of ITALIAN BREAD on each dinner plate.
39. Use tongs to serve PASTA and SHRIMP to each dinner plate.
40. Grab handful of PARMESAN CHEESE and sprinkle over plate #1. Repeat for plate #2.
41. Carry dinner plates to table.
42. Dinner is served!

Post-dinner Note: The garlic/shrimp combo will <u>stink up</u> your apartment, so make sure you – at the very least – <u>rinse off</u> the *plates* before you go to bed. You'll be glad you did in the morning!

PASTA & PIZZA

Btw, "Al Dente" means "not mushy." Al Dente is how they cook pasta in Italy.

"Just What The Doctor Ordered" Pasta

Dr. Mary Harder is another one of *those* people: good at everything. Ranked #1 in her med school class. Fakies with air on her wake board. And she removes all the pre-cancerous lesions from my "cheap Irish skin" – my 100% German mother's phrase – for free!!!

This meal lives up to its name. And it is delicious, to boot.

Ease: 1 Chef
Cost: $53
Preparation Time: 5 minutes
Cooking Time: 40 minutes (20 of which are waiting for the pasta water to boil)

Ingredients:
Ground Beef – 1 pound; $4.69
Rotini – 1 sixteen-ounce Box; $2.75 (*Rotini is a lot more fun than spaghetti, But you can use whatever pasta you like best*)
Spicy Italian Sausage – 3; $3.38 for package of 5
Tomato Soup – 1 Can; $1.69
Cream of Mushroom Soup – 1 Can; $1.69
Sea Salt – 1 TEAspoon; $3.99
Cracked Black Pepper – 1 TEAspoon; $3.99
Olive Oil – 2 TABLEspoons; $6-13 per bottle
Shredded Parmesan Cheese – 1 sixteen-ounce Bag; $3.99
Salad – 1 Bag pre-washed; $5
Tomatoes – 2; $2.99 per pound
Salad Dressing – Bottle of your choice; $2
Take-n-Bake Garlic Bread – 1 Loaf; $2.00 (*Found in Bakery section of super market*)
Butter – 4 TABLEspoons; $5.50 per 4 sticks

Recommended Wine: Cabernet or, if feeling adventurous, Syrah

Tools, etc:
Large Pasta Pot
Frying Pan – Large
Paring Knife
Small Plate – 2
Cutting Board
Wooden Spoon
Paper Towels

Colander (the thingy with all the holes; it's for draining things)
Oven Mitts
Stopwatch
Large Serving Bowl

Directions:
1. 30 minutes before you want to eat, fill large pasta pot with WATER AMOUNT specified in pasta directions.
2. Place large pasta pot on rear stovetop burner and crank flame to high heat. Cover pot.
3. Unwrap 3 SAUSAGES. (You can freeze the other SAUSAGES or keep them in the fridge and cook them within 3 days)
4. Use paring knife to slice off SAUSAGE CASINGS.
5. Throw out casings.
6. On small plate #1, slice SAUSAGES into ¼" thick PIECES.
7. Slice 4 TABLEspoons of BUTTER (Use the ruler on the wax paper wrapper to measure this) and add to small plate #2 for later use.
8. Put colander in sink.
9. Open BAG OF SALAD. Add SALAD to salad bowls.
10. On cutting board, slice TOMATOES. Throw out TOPS and BOTTOMS of TOMATOES.
11. Run WATER in sink. Rinse off icky, green SEEDS from TOMATOES. Then, drop TOMATOES into colander to dry.
12. Preheat oven to temperature specified on BREAD BAG.
13. Set oven timer for 5 minutes.
14. Unwrap GROUND BEEF.
15. Place large frying pan on front stovetop burner.
16. When oven timer goes off, open TAKE-N-BAKE GARLIC BREAD.
17. Put on oven mitt. Open oven door. Slide out rack.
18. Place BREAD on rack.
19. Slide in rack. Close oven door. Take off oven mitt.
20. Set oven timer for time specified on BREAD BAG (usually @ 15 min).
21. When WATER in pasta pot finally boils, add 6 shakes of SEA SALT.
22. Add Box of PASTA. Stir with wooden spoon.
23. Set stopwatch for amount of time listed on PASTA BOX.
24. Crank flame under frying pan to high heat.
25. Put 2 handfuls of PARMESAN CHEESE in a bowl for later.
26. Measure 2 TABLEspoons of OLIVE OIL and add to frying pan.

27. When OLIVE OIL begins to slide around easily, add CHOPPED SAUSAGES and GROUND BEEF.
28. Use a wooden spoon to continuously turn over MEAT so it browns with no red left.
29. Once the MEAT is brown, add 1 Can of TOMATO SOUP.
30. Add 1 Can of CREAM OF MUSHROOM SOUP.
31. Gently stir the SOUPS in with the MEAT. Warning: Tomato and Cream of Mushroom do not play well together, so this could take a lot of stirring.
32. When the MEAT SAUCE boils, lower flame under frying pan to low.
33. Stir occasionally as the MEAT SAUCE simmers. Be sure to scrape off the CRUSTY STUFF on the side of the frying pan and work it back into the general population.
34. Beware the dreaded "Stovetop Lean." You know how "experienced" pool tables lean more to one side than the other? Old stovetops can do the same thing, causing the contents of frying pans to fill higher on one side. This is a potential nuclear disaster waiting to happen. Pay attention to your pan! You might have to jury rig a spoon on one side to balance things out. Do NOT use anything flammable to do the balancing.
35. Rinse out the CANS you just emptied and chuck them in your recycling bin. Remember, Ms. Right Now wants you to A.B.R. – Always Be Recycling!
36. When timer goes off, turn off oven.
37. Put on oven mitt. Open oven door. Slide out bottom rack.
38. Remove BREAD and place on cutting board.
39. Slide in rack. Close oven door. Take off oven mitt.
40. Add TOMATOES to salad bowls.
41. Rinse out colander. Keep it in sink.
42. When stopwatch goes off, turn off flame under pasta pot.
43. Put on oven mitts.
44. Carry pasta pot to sink and pour PASTA and WATER into colander.
45. Shake colander several times to aid the draining.
46. Place large serving bowl next to sink.
47. Turn off flame under frying pan.
48. Carry butter plate, cheese bowl and salad bowls to table.
49. Pour PASTA into large serving bowl.
50. Dump handful of PARMESAN CHEESE on top of PASTA.
51. Carefully pour MEAT SAUCE on top of PASTA.
52. Dump handful of PARMESAN CHEESE on top of MEAT SAUCE.
53. Take wooden spoon and thoroughly stir SAUCE and PASTA until CHEESE melts.

54. Spoon PASTA and MEAT SAUCE onto dinner plates.
55. Slice ¼ Loaf of BREAD. Put 2 SLICES on each dinner plate.
56. Carry dinner plates to table.
57. Dinner is served!

JB's Salsa Spaghetti

Jeff Brunner owns a successful company and has a cute wife; he's doing something right. This recipe provides a spicy, easy twist to good ol' spaghetti.

Ease: 1 Chef
Cost: $46
Preparation Time: 5 minutes
Cooking Time: 40 minutes (includes time to boil water)

Ingredients:
Spaghetti – 1 Box (16 ounces); $2.55
Ground Turkey – 1 pound; $5
Prego Sauce – 1 jar; $3.19
Fresh Salsa – 1 container of medium or spicy; $2.99 (*Not a standard jar! This is the perishable stuff found in the refrigerated section of the market*)
Shredded Mozzarella Cheese – 1 sixteen-ounce bag; $4.99
Sea Salt – 6 shakes; $3.99 per bottle
Extra Virgin Olive Oil – 2 TABLEspoons; $6-13 depending on brand
Mrs. Dash seasoning – 3 shakes; $3.99
Cholula Hot Sauce; $3.29 (*Use this for an extra kick; however, you should know Beforehand if she likes it super hot. A scorched mouth won't lead to scorching sex*)
Shredded Parmesan Cheese – 1 sixteen-ounce bag; $3.99 (*not the Green Can that's been in your parents' fridge your whole life; get the fresh stuff*)
Salad – 1 Bag pre-washed; $5
Tomatoes – 2; $2.99 per pound
Salad Dressing – Bottle of your choice; $2
Take-n-Bake Garlic Bread – 1 Loaf; $2.00 (*Found in Bakery section of market*)

Recommended Wine: Merlot or, if feeling adventurous, Dolcetto

Tools, etc:
Large Pasta Pot
Colander (the thingy with all the holes; it's for draining pasta)
Large Frying Pan
Measuring Spoons
Sauce Pot
Wooden Spoon
Stopwatch
Tongs

Directions:

1. 30 minutes before you want to eat, add 6 quarts of WATER to the large pasta pot and place pot on a burner over a high flame. Cover pot. It should take 20-25 minutes for the water to boil.
2. Place colander in sink.
3. Place frying pan on burner. Turn flame to medium.
4. Measure 2 TABLEspoons of OLIVE OIL and add to frying pan.
5. When the OIL starts sliding easily all over the pan, add GROUND TURKEY to frying pan.
6. Use a wooden spoon to continuously turn over TURKEY so it browns with no red left, but does not burn.
7. When the TURKEY is done, turn off flame.
8. Place saucepot on a second burner.
9. Add jar of PREGO SAUCE to saucepot.
10. Measure 6 TABLEspoons of SALSA and add to saucepot.
11. 3 shakes of MRS. DASH.
12. Use wooden spoon to stir.
13. Add TURKEY to saucepot. Stir again.
14. Pre-heat oven to temperature specified on BREAD BAG.
15. Set oven timer for 5 minutes.
16. Wash TOMATOES. Pat dry with paper towels.
17. Rinse out the JAR you just emptied and chuck it in your recycling bin. Remember, Ms. Right Now wants you to A.B.R. – Always Be Recycling!
18. Open BAG OF SALAD. Add SALAD to salad bowls.
19. Slice TOMATOES. Throw out TOPS and BOTTOMS of TOMATOES.
20. Run WATER in sink. Rinse off icky, green SEEDS from TOMATOES. Then, drop TOMATOES into colander to dry.
21. When oven timer goes off, open TAKE-N-BAKE BREAD.
22. Put on oven mitt. Open oven door. Slide out rack.
23. Place BREAD on rack.
24. Slide in rack. Close oven door. Take off oven mitt.
25. Re-set oven timer for time specified on BREAD BAG (usually @ 15 min).
26. When WATER in pasta pot boils, add 6 shakes of SALT.
27. Add SPAGHETTI. Set stopwatch for time specified on PASTA BOX.
28. Turn on medium flame under the saucepot.

29. When the sauce begins simmering, sprinkle in 2 palmfuls (this is the scientific term) of MOZZARELLA CHEESE.
30. Stir as CHEESE melts into SAUCE.
31. Once cheese has completely melted, turn off flame.
32. If you want the sauce spicier, add a few drops of CHOLULA HOT SAUCE.
33. Add TOMATOES to salad bowls.
34. Rinse out colander. Leave colander in sink.
35. Stir PASTA.
36. Put 2 handfuls of SHREDDED PARMESAN CHEESE in bowl.
37. Add SALAD DRESSING to salad.
38. Cut 4 TABLEspoons of BUTTER (Use the ruler on the wax paper wrapper to measure this) and place on small plate.
39. When stopwatch goes off, turn off flame under PASTA.
40. Put on oven mitts and carefully carry pasta pot to sink.
41. Pour WATER and PASTA into colander. Let the pasta drain.
42. Take off oven mitts.
43. When oven timer goes off, turn off oven.
44. Put on oven mitt. Open oven door. Slide out rack.
45. Remove BREAD and place on cutting board.
46. Slide in rack. Close oven door. Take off oven mitt.
47. Carry salad bowls, butter plate and cheese bowl to table.
48. Use tongs to put the SPAGHETTI onto dinner plates. Cover SPAGHETTI with SAUCE.
49. Slice ¼ Loaf of BREAD and place 2 slices on each dinner plate.
50. Carry spaghetti plates to the table.
51. Dinner is served!

EJ's "Reverse Cowboy" Barbeque Chicken Pizza

EJ Strittmater is an annoying guy; chicks drool over him, he makes a killing in real estate and he cooks, too. Fortunately, he's an Ohio State fan, so I have a legit reason to hate his guts.

I had no idea making pizza was so easy. You can make two at a time - one on each rack of the oven – and freeze the second.

Ease: 1 Chef
Cost: $32

Preparation Time: 70 minutes (Includes thaw time for chicken)
Cooking Time: 15 minutes (Including 5 minutes of cooling time)

Ingredients:
Boboli Pizza Crust – 1; $3.89
Frozen Pre-cooked Chicken Strips – 1 package; $8.29
Hickory Barbeque Sauce – 1 cup; $2.00
Buffalo Chicken Seasoning – 1 package; $2.29 (*Found in the same section of supermarket as French Onion Soup mix*)
Shredded Mozzarella Cheese – 1 sixteen-ounce package; $4.99
Pre-washed Salad – 1 bag; $5.00
Tomatoes – 2; $2.99 per pound
Salad Dressing – 1 bottle of your choice; $2.00

Recommended Wine: Beer or, if feeling Grey Poupon-y, Zinfandel

Tools, etc:
Tin Foil
Plastic 2-gallon Freezer Bag – 1
Colander
Measuring Cup
Oven Mitt – 2
Spatulas – 2
Pizza Platter
Pizza slicing wheel

Directions:

1. 90 minutes before you want to eat, place CHICKEN BAG on counter to thaw.
2. Open oven door. Slide out BOTTOM rack.
3. Grab tin foil. Cover bottom rack with tin foil. This will keep the cheese that drips off the pizza from burning on the bottom rack and/or oven floor and setting off your fire alarm every time you cook.
4. Pre-heat oven to 450 degrees.
5. Put colander in sink.
6. Pour 1 packet of BUFFALON CHICKEN SEASONING into ziploc bag.
7. Add CHICKEN STRIPS to ziploc bag. Seal bag.
8. Shake Ziploc bag like crazy until STRIPS are covered in seasoning.
9. Remove PIZZA CRUST from package.
10. Measure 1 cup of BARBEQUE SAUCE and pour onto PIZZA CRUST.
11. With a spoon, spread SAUCE onto every inch of CRUST, making sure to leave room at the edges for the, uh, crust.
12. Open MOZARELLA CHEESE. Spread CHEESE all over crust.

13. Open Ziploc bag. Place seasoned STRIPS all over crust.
14. Put on oven mitt. Open oven door. Slide out top rack.
15. Place PIZZA on rack. Slide in. Close door. Take off oven mitts.
16. Set oven timer for 10 minutes.
17. On the cutting board chop TOMATOES. Throw out TOPS and BOTTOMS of TOMATOES.
18. Run WATER in sink. Rinse off icky, green SEEDS from TOMATOES. Then, drop TOMATOES into colander to dry.
19. Add SALAD to salad bowls.
20. Place platter on counter next to oven.
21. When oven timer goes off, turn off oven.
22. Put on oven mitts. Open door. Slide out rack.
23. Using spatulas, pick up PIZZA and place on top of platter.
24. Set oven timer for 5 minutes, to give pizza time to cool.
25. Add TOMATOES to salad bowls.
26. Add SALAD DRESSING to SALAD.
27. Carry salad bowls to table.
28. When oven timer goes off, cut PIZZA with pizza wheel.
29. Carry pizza platter to table.
30. Dinner is served!

Marisa's Mexican Lasagna

If this meal turns out half as good as Marisa Rendall looks, then you are golden!
    This recipe combines some Italian and Mexican staples. It's made like a lasagna, but will turn out more like an enchilada. You'll see what I mean when you dig in.
    I added to Marisa's recipe because I thought it needed some "oomph." She undoubtedly felt the same about me when we dated.

Ease: 4 Chefs (Only because it's tedious to assemble the three layers.)
Cost: $56
Preparation Time: 30 minutes
Cooking Time: 50 minutes, total, including 5 minutes for cool down.

Ingredients:
Cubed Chicken Breasts – 32 ounces; $6.99 per 20-ounce bag
Corn Tortillas – 18; $1.89 per package of 24
Marinara Sauce – 12-ounces; $3.00 per sixteen-ounce jar
Spicy Taco Sauce – 1 packet; .60 cents. (*You will find this in the same section*

As Hot Wings Seasoning, Gravy, etc)
Black Beans – 2 Cans; .99 per 14-ounce can
Canned Corn – 2 Cans; .50 per 11-ounce can
Shredded "Mexican" Cheese – 24-ounces; $3.50 per 16-ounce bag (*This may also be called "4-Cheese". It's 4 different "Mexican" cheeses mixed together: Monterey Jack, Cheddar, Queso Quesadilla and Asadero*)
Salt – 3 TEAspoons; $2.19 per bottle
Black Pepper – 3 TEAspoons; $2.19 per bottle
Bag of Pre-washed Salad; 5.00
Tomatoes – 4; $2.99 per pound
Salad Dressing – 1 bottle of your choice; $2.00

Recommended Wine: Cabernet or, if feeling adventurous, Syrah

Tools, etc:
Saucepot
Paring Knife
Measuring Cup
Measuring Spoons
Oven Mitt
Large Baking Dish
Dinner Spoon
Colander (The thingy with all the holes; it's for draining stuff in the sink)
Paper Towels
Spatula

Directions:

1. Separate TORTILLAS from the pile.
2. Individually place TORTILLAS in saucepot by slightly overlapping them clockwise.
3. Fill saucepot halfway with HOT WATER.
4. Set oven timer for 5 minutes. This will soften up the tortillas.
5. Place colander in sink.
6. Wash TOMATOES. Dry TOMATOES with paper towel.
7. On the cutting board, chop TOMATOES. Throw out TOPS and BOTTOMS of TOMATOES.
8. Run WATER in sink. Rinse off icky, green SEEDS from TOMATOES.
9. Drop CHOPPED TOMATOES in colander to dry.
10. Place large baking dish on counter so it's parallel to you.
11. In the measuring cup, measure 6 ounces of MARINARA SAUCE and pour into large baking dish.
12. Cover every spot on the bottom of the large baking dish with MARINARA.
13. When oven timer goes off, pour out saucepot WATER into sink.

14. Grab a TORTILLA and shake off any remaining WATER.
15. Place TORTILLA on top of the SAUCE in the upper right corner of the baking dish.
16. Shake the water off 1 more TORTILLA.
17. Place TORTILLA to the left of the first, thus covering the upper portion of the baking dish.
18. Shake the water off 2 TORTILLAS.
19. Place TORTILLAS in matching positions in the middle portion of the baking dish.
20. Shake the water off 2 TORTILLAS.
21. Place TORTILLAS in matching positions in lower portion of baking dish.
22. Empty ½ packet of SPICY TACO POWDER into 1 can of BLACK BEANS.
23. Empty remaining ½ packet into other can of BEANS.
24. Stir the MIXTURES with the dinner spoon.
25. In the measuring cup, measure 7 ounces of CORN.
26. Use dinner spoon to spread CORN equally across the TORTILLAS.
27. In the measuring cup, measure 9 ounces of BLACK BEANS.
28. Use dinner spoon to spread BEANS equally across the TORTILLAS.
29. In the measuring cup, measure 9 ounces of MEXICAN CHEESE.
30. Using your fingers, sprinkle CHEESE equally across the TORTILLAS.
31. Fill measuring spoon with 1 TEAspoon of SALT.
32. Take a pinch and sprinkle SALT equally over a TORTILLA.
33. Repeat pinch and sprinkle for rest of TORTILLAS in baking dish.
34. Fill measuring spoon with 1 TEAspoon of PEPPER.
35. Take a pinch and sprinkle SALT equally over a TORTILLA.
36. Repeat pinch and sprinkle for rest of TORTILLAS in baking dish.
37. In the measuring cup, measure 10 ounces of CHICKEN.
38. Using your fingers, place CHICKEN equally across the TORTILLAS. Note: Try to make sure the edges all have CHICKEN on them, as this will help prop up the other two levels of tortillas and keep them from drooping.
39. Grab a TORTILLA and shake off any remaining WATER.
40. Place TORTILLA on top of CHICKEN in upper right corner of baking dish.
41. Shake the water off 1 more TORTILLA.
42. Place TORTILLA to the left of the first, thus covering the upper portion of the baking dish.
43. Shake the water off 2 TORTILLAS.
44. Place TORTILLAS in matching positions on the middle portion of the baking dish.

45. Shake the water off 2 TORTILLAS.
46. Place TORTILLAS in matching positions on the LOWER portion of the baking dish.
47. Repeat steps 25 – 38.
48. Preheat oven to 350 degrees.
49. Grab a TORTILLA and shake off any remaining WATER.
50. Place TORTILLA on top of the CHICKEN in the upper right corner of the baking dish.
51. Shake the water off 1 more TORTILLA.
52. Place TORTILLA to the left of the first, thus covering the upper portion of the baking dish.
53. Shake the water off 2 TORTILLAS.
54. Place TORTILLAS in matching positions on the middle portion of the baking dish.
55. Shake the water off 2 TORTILLAS.
56. Place TORTILLAS in matching positions on the lower portion of the baking dish.
57. Repeat steps 25 – 38.
58. In the measuring cup, measure 6 ounces of MARINARA SAUCE.
59. Spread MARINARA across top of CHICKEN.
60. Sprinkle remaining CHEESE on top of MARINARA.
61. Put on oven mitt. Open oven door. Slide out rack.
62. Place baking dish on rack. Slide in rack. Close door. Take off oven mitt.
63. Set oven timer for 45 minutes.
64. Rinse out the CANS you just emptied and chuck them in your recycling bin. Remember, Ms. Right Now wants you to A.B.R. – Always Be Recycling!
65. When oven timer goes off, turn off oven.
66. Put on oven mitt. Open oven door. Slide out rack.
67. Place baking dish on cool oven burners.
68. Open BAG OF SALAD.
69. Place SALAD in bowls.
70. Add TOMATOES to salads.
71. Add SALAD DRESSING to salads.
72. Using spatula, cut two 3 x 4 inch SERVINGS.
73. Place SERVINGS on each dinner plate.
74. Carry salad bowls and dinner plates to table.
75. Dinner is served!

Chef Zach's Lasagna Bolognese

For those of you who have yet to try Chef Zach's Swordfish recipe, uh, what are you waiting for?

Zach has done it again.

First of all, "Bolognese" does not mean "Lasagna with baloney." You will not be adding any Oscar Mayer slices, here. "Bolognese" indicates the recipe originates from Bologna, a town in northern Italy. Nowadays, Bolognese means any Italian-style meat and pasta sauce.

I'm not gonna lie to you…lasagna is a lot of work. Fortunately, since every girl on Earth knows how much effort this Italian feast requires, it will be well worth your efforts. Also, you'll have enough leftovers to last you – or your cheapskate roommates – for a week.

Zach suggests preparing the lasagna the night before the date – think of it as the cooking equivalent of making a restaurant reservation. This'll save you a lot of time the day of the date, which could come in handy if the apartment cleaning takes longer than anticipated.

Note: Zach – and every cookbook on Earth – recommends cooking the noodles first. You do <u>not</u> have to do this, thanks to the lazy genius who invented "oven ready" lasagna noodles!

Ease: 4 Chefs
Cost: $63
Preparation Time: 90 minutes
Cooking Time: 30 minutes (with 10 minutes to cool)

Ingredients:
"Oven Ready" Lasagna Flat Pasta – 1 sixteen-ounce Box; $4.00
Ground Beef – 2 Pounds (can be lean or not); $6.00 for lean, $2.75 for regular
Whole, peeled Tomatoes – Two 28-ounce Cans; $2.19 per can
Ricotta Cheese – 2 Pints; $4.19 per pint *(Note: Ricotta is found in the refrigerated supermarket section with fresh, packaged ravioli)*
Grated Parmesan Cheese – 2 16-ounce packages; $2.99 – 3.89 per package
Fresh Basil – 2 packages; $1.99 per package

You can do the GARLIC the difficult – but more impressive – way or the easy way. Just depends on whether you want to make like mob boss Paulie in the prison scenes from "Goodfellas" and slice your own garlic, or not. Your fingers will stink.

<u>Difficult</u> Garlic – 2 Heads; .99 cents per head (*The head or bulb is the whole, bumpy thing; a "clove" is one of the Bumps*)
<u>Easy</u> Garlic – 3 TABLEspoons + 1 TEAspoon of Minced; $2.49 per jar
Extra Virgin Olive Oil – 8 TABLEspoons divided $6-13 per bottle *("Divided" means you'll use them separately)*;
Sea Salt – 1.5 TEAspoons divided; $3.99 per bottle
Salad – 1 bag of pre-washed; $5
Tomatoes – 2; $2.99 per pound
Salad Dressing – Your Choice; $2 per bottle
Take-n-Bake Garlic Bread – 1 Loaf; $2.00
Non-Stick Spray – $4.00

Recommended Wine: Cabernet or, if feeling adventurous, Chianti

Tools, etc:
Small Plate
Large Baking Dish
Large Frying Pan – 1
Measuring Cup – 1
Measuring Spoons
Tinfoil
Timer or stopwatch – 1
Cutting Board
Colander (The thingy with all the holes in it; it's for draining stuff in the sink)
Large Salad Bowl – 1
Regular Salad Bowl – 2
Oven Mitt
Wooden Spoon
Spatula

Directions:

REGARDLESS of whether you are following Chef Zach's recommendation and cooking this the night *before* the date, or are staying true to your clueless bachelor roots and winging it the day of, the preparation of the LASAGNA is the same!

1. Go with whichever GARLIC method you picked. So, either peel and slice 2 heads of GARLIC or measure 3 TABLEspoons + 1 TEAspoon MINCED GARLIC onto a small plate.
2. Place large frying pan on burner.
3. Measure 5 TABLEspoons of OLIVE OIL and add to large frying pan.
4. Turn on flame to low.
5. Scrape GARLIC into large frying pan.
6. Set oven timer for 30 seconds. Keep an eye on the pan to be sure not to burn the garlic! Burnt garlic tastes bitter.
7. Rinse off small plate and wipe dry with paper towel. You'll need plate later.
8. When oven timer goes off, crank up the flame under large frying pan.
9. Add the GROUND BEEF to the pan. (Note: if you drop in the beef directly from the package, make sure you remove the sticky paper that is stuck to the bottom of the beef. Don't ask how I know to do that.)
10. Set oven timer for 6 minutes.
11. Use wooden spoon to stir the MIXTURE frequently. The purpose here is to brown the beef, not cook hamburgers.
12. Open one TOMATO CAN.
13. Reach into CAN, grab a WHOLE TOMATO…and start crushing! Seriously. You need to crush all the tomatoes. You may be wondering, like I was, "Why not just BUY a can of

crushed tomatoes?" Zach explains, "At the giant factory, the best tomatoes make it through the process intact and go in the Whole Tomato bin, while the substandard ones – Cough. Losers! – get chucked into the Crushed Tomato bin."

14. When you've crushed all the tomatoes in CAN #1, repeat for CAN #2.
15. When the oven timer goes off, dump the CANS into the large frying pan. (That is, dump the CONTENTS of the cans, not the cans themselves.)
16. Stir the SAUCE thoroughly to mix it all up.
17. When the MIXTURE boils, reduce the flame to low.
18. Set oven timer for 30 minutes. (Note: If you sample a taste from the wooden spoon, don't be surprised if the sauce isn't "right." It needs the salt you're gonna add later. Trust me.)
19. Place BASIL on small plate. Cut off STEMS.
20. Set aside 3 BASIL BRANCHES. You'll use them later to complete LASAGNA.
21. Rip up the remaining BASIL. This is a great stress reliever.
22. Stir SAUCE.
23. Stir SAUCE.
24. You guessed it. Stir SAUCE.
25. When oven timer goes off, turn off flame. Let SAUCE cool.
26. Finally! You get to work the large baking dish.
27. Measure 3 TABLEspoons of OLIVE OIL and add to the baking dish.
28. Pick up large baking dish and tilt it up and down to swirl the OLIVE OIL around so that the entire dish is covered.
29. Place large baking dish on counter so it is parallel to you.
30. Use your fingers to make sure every inch is oiled up. Wipe your fingers with paper towels, Greasy Guy.
31. Open the LASAGNA BOX.
32. Take out 1 NOODLE and lay it horizontally across the baking dish. Be sure to abut the left NOODLE EDGE against the northern most side of the dish. You might have to break off the piece so it fits nicely within the dish walls. Put the SCRAPS on the side, as you might need them later.
33. Pick up another NOODLE and lay it parallel to his brother, just like you're laying two-by-fours when building a deck.
34. Repeat the process until the bottom of the dish is totally covered.
35. Open 1 pint of the RICOTTA CHEESE.
36. In the measuring cup, measure 10 ounces of RICOTTA.

37. Spoon out and spread RICOTTA evenly over the NOODLES, like you're icing a cake (not that I've ever done that). You might find that you have an adversarial relationship with the ricotta. You are not crazy; it's the cheese's fault.
38. Grab the frying pan in one hand and grab the wooden spoon with your other.
39. Spoon approximately 1/3 of the MEAT SAUCE onto the RICOTTA. Again, make sure the SAUCE spreads evenly across the PASTA.
40. With the measuring spoon, measure ½ TEAspoon of SEA SALT.
41. With your fingers, sprinkle SALT evenly on top of the MEAT SAUCE.
42. In the measuring cup, measure 10 ounces of PARMESAN CHEESE.
43. With your fingers, sprinkle PARMESAN evenly on top of the SALT. (Note: when you are done building the lasagna, you will still have 2 ounces of PARMESAN left. You'll need it.)
44. Grab approximately 1/3 of the ripped up BASIL.
45. With your fingers, sprinkle BASIL evenly on top of the PARMESAN.
46. Time to start building the second floor of your lasagna house.
47. Repeat steps 32 – 45. Noodles, ricotta, meat sauce, sea salt, parmesan and basil.
48. Third floor, dude! Repeat steps 32 – 45. Noodles, ricotta, meat sauce, sea salt, parmesan and basil.

STOP! If you are preparing this the DAY OF the date, <u>pre-heat</u> the *oven* to **450 degrees**. If you are following Zach's suggestion and doing it the day before, don't do anything to the *oven*.

1. Once the LASAGNA'S third floor is done, you should be looking down at exposed MEAT SAUCE, PARMESAN and BASIL.
2. Cover baking dish in tinfoil.
3. Rinse out the CANS and PLASTIC you just emptied and chuck them in your recycling bin. Remember, Ms. Right Now wants you to A.B.R. – Always Be Recycling!

STOP! If you are doing it the night before, <u>store</u> *baking dish* in *fridge*.
"Night Before" Guys, you will have to <u>pre-heat</u> the *oven* to **450 degrees** prior to baking LASAGNA.
Regardless of when you're preparing the lasagna, follow these next directions to bake it.

4. Put on oven mitts. Open oven door and slide out top rack.
5. Place baking dish on rack. Slide in top rack. Close door. Take off oven mitts.
6. Set oven timer for 15 minutes.
7. Open BAG OF SALAD. Add to salad bowls.
8. Wash TOMATOES. Dry TOMATOES with paper towel.
9. Place colander in sink.

10. On cutting board, slice TOMATOES. Throw out both the tops and bottoms of TOMATOES.
11. Turn on WATER in sink. Take SLICED TOMATOES in your fingers and rinse off the icky, green SEEDS. Then, drop clean TOMATOES into colander to dry.
12. When the oven timer goes off, open TAKE-N-BAKE GARLIC BREAD.
13. Put on oven mitt. Open oven door and slide out bottom rack.
14. Place GARLIC BREAD on bottom rack.
15. Slide in bottom rack. Close door. Take off oven mitt.
16. Reset oven timer for 5 minutes.
17. Add equal amounts of SLICED TOMATOES to salad bowls.
18. When oven timer goes off, put on oven mitts.
19. Open oven door and slide out top rack.
20. Remove large baking dish and move it onto unlit burners.
21. Slide in top rack. Close oven door.
22. Reduce oven temperature to whatever temperature is listed in BREAD BAG INSTRUCTIONS.
23. Reset oven timer for the remaining amount of time needed to cook bread as listed on BREAD BAG INSTRUCTIONS. Remember: you already used 5 minutes.
24. Remove tinfoil from large baking dish. Throw out tinfoil.
25. When oven timer goes off, turn off oven.
26. Put on oven mitts. Open oven door. Slide out bottom rack.
27. Remove GARLIC BREAD and place on cutting board.
28. Slide in rack. Close oven door.
29. Add SALAD DRESSING to SALAD.
30. Carry salad bowls and butter plate to table.
31. Slice ¼ of GARLIC BREAD. Place 2 slices on each dinner plate.
32. Sprinkle remaining PARMESAN all over LASAGNA.
33. Pick up remaining BASIL and sprinkle all over LASAGNA.
34. Use spatula to cut 3" x 3" square of LASAGNA and lift square onto dinner plate.
35. Repeat for step 80 for other dinner plate.
36. Carry dinner plates to table.
37. Dinner is served!

COMMIE PINKO, ER, VEGETARIAN ENTREES

Ammo's 6-Can Veggie Chili

My sister is getting a great birthday present this year!

This recipe is perfect for a vegetarian Ms. Right Now. I was shocked by this meal's tastiness. Seriously, I could barely tell there wasn't any beef or chicken in it.

This chili freezes well AND it will keep in the fridge up to one week, thanks to its lack of meat.

My sister says the chili is better if you cook it the day before and then store it in the fridge for 24 hours. I ignored her and ate it one hour after cooking it – still tasted great. Your call.

Ease: 1 Chef
Cost: $64
Preparation Time: 5 minutes
Cooking Time: 30 minutes

Ingredients:
Extra Virgin Olive Oil – 1 TABLEspoon; $6-13
Black Beans – one 15-ounce Can; 67 cents
Garbanzo Beans (a.k.a. Chickpeas) – one 15-ounce Can; 79 cents
Red Kidney Beans – one 15-ounce Can; 79 cents
Corn Kernels – one 11-ounce Can; 69 cents (*Make sure it's not a can of CREAMED corn!*)
Crushed Tomatoes – one 28-ounce Can; $2.88
Tomato Paste – one 6-ounce Can; 50 cents
Yellow Bell Pepper – 1; $1.50 per pound
Red Bell Pepper – 1; $1.50 per pound
Yellow Onion – 1 (it may look more brown than yellow); $1.29 per pound
Chili Powder – 4 TABLEspoons; $6.69 per bottle
Oregano – 2 TABLEspoons; $4.99 per bottle
Sea Salt – 1 TABLEspoon; $3.99 per bottle
Cracked Black Pepper – 1 TABLEspoon; $3.99 per bottle
White Rice – 1 Microwavable Bag; $2.49
Pre-washed Salad – 1 Bag; $5.00
Tomatoes – 2; $2.99 per pound
Salad Dressing – 1 bottle of your choice; $2.00
Shredded Cheddar Cheese – one 16-ounce bag; $3.39
Sour Cream – one 16-ounce container; $1–3.00
Tortilla Chips – 1 Bag; $3.50
Oyster Crackers – 1 box; $3.00 (*Since you won't know whether she prefers*

tortilla chips or Oyster Crackers with her chili, it's smart to have both)

Recommended Wine: Chardonnay or, if feeling adventurous, Primativo (which is Italian Zinfandel)

Tools, etc:
Colander (The thingy with all the holes; it's for draining stuff in the sink)
Large Mixing Bowl
Paper Towels
Can Opener
Measuring Spoons
Medium Mixing Bowl
Cutting Board
Paring Knife
Metal Spoon
Large Pasta Pot
Oven Mittens (2)
Wooden Spoon
Small Bowls – 2
Serving Bowls – 3

Directions:

1. Place colander in sink.
2. Place large mixing bowl next to sink.
3. Place large pasta pot on stove top burner. Don't light flame!
4. Wash RED and YELLOW BELL PEPPERS. Pat dry with paper towels.
5. Use can opener to open BLACK BEANS, GARBANZO BEANS, RED KIDNEY BEANS and CORN KERNELS.
6. Pour BLACK BEANS into colander to drain the nasty goop that is used in the canning process.
7. Dump BLACK BEANS from colander into large mixing bowl.
8. Rinse out colander.
9. Repeat steps 4-6 for the GARBANZO BEANS, RED KIDNEY BEANS and CORN KERNELS.
10. Rinse out the CANS you just emptied and chuck them in your recycling bin. Remember, Ms. Right Now wants you to A.B.R. – Always Be Recycling!
11. Measure 1 TABLEspoon of OLIVE OIL and add it to large pasta pot.
12. Clean out MEASURING SPOON with a paper towel.
13. Cut open top of RED BELL PEPPER. Pull out and throw out STEM. Shake out SEEDS into trash.

14. On the cutting board, slice RED BELL PEPPER in half. Shake out any remaining SEEDS into trash. Cut out and throw out all WHITE PARTS inside pepper.
15. Chop up RED BELL PEPPER into half-inch wide sections. Next, chop those into 1/8" x 1/8" strips, a.k.a. about the size of the onions on a McDonald's hamburger.
16. Add RED BELL PEPPER to medium mixing bowl.
17. Repeat steps 11-14 for YELLOW BELL PEPPER.
18. Turn on oven exhaust fan.
19. This is totally serious: Put a metal spoon in your mouth. This will help keep you from crying while chopping onions.
20. Chop off both ends of ONION. Peel the SKIN off the ONION. Peel 1 layer off the ONION.
21. Slice ONION in half. Look for a thin TUBE of onion in the center. Throw that piece in trash.
22. Chop ONION into 1/8" x 1/8" PIECES.
23. Add CHOPPED ONION to medium mixing bowl.
24. Turn on flame to low-medium heat under large pasta pot.
25. Add PEPPERS and ONIONS to large pasta pot.
26. Set oven timer for 7 minutes.
27. Stir PEPPERS and ONIONS every minute. The ONIONS will turn translucent.
28. Use can opener to open CRUSHED TOMATOES.
29. When the timer goes off, add CONTENTS of the large mixing bowl to the large pasta pot.
30. Pour ENTIRE CAN of CRUSHED TOMATOES into large pasta pot.
31. Open CHILI POWDER bottle. Very carefully – if you do it too fast, your kitchen's gonna be covered in brown dust.
32. Remove the plastic top. (Otherwise, it'll take forever to pour out the required amount).
33. Throw out plastic top. Why? Because it's useless and it feels really good to chuck something forced on you by The Man!
34. Measure 4 TABLEspoons of CHILI POWDER and add to the pasta pot.
35. Measure 2 TABLEspoons of OREGANO and add to the pasta pot.
36. Measure 1 TABLEspoons of SEA SALT and add to the pasta pot.
37. Measure 1 TABLEspoons of BLACK PEPPER and add to the pasta pot.
38. Stir all INGREDIENTS in pasta pot with the wooden spoon.
39. Crank flame to high heat.
40. When CHILI boils, lower flame to the original low-medium heat.

41. Set oven timer for 30 minutes. Stir CHILI every 5 minutes with the wooden spoon. When stirring, be sure to scrape the bottom of the pot to avoid having a layer of burnt stuff.
42. Rinse out the CANS you just emptied and chuck them in your recycling bin. Remember, Ms. Right Now wants you to A.B.R. – Always Be Recycling!

If making the night before the date, postpone salad-making **steps 40-45** till tomorrow night.

1. Wash TOMATOES. Pat dry with paper towels.
2. Place colander in sink.
3. On cutting board, slice TOMATOES. Throw out both the tops and bottoms of TOMATOES.
4. Turn on WATER in sink. Take SLICED TOMATOES in your fingers and rinse off the icky, green SEEDS.
5. Drop clean TOMATOES into colander to dry.
6. Open SALAD BAG. Add SALAD to two salad bowls.
7. When oven timer goes off, turn off flame. Move pasta pot to a cool burner.

If making the night before the date, pour the CHILI into a *large serving bowl* and cover with *tin foil*. Then, place the *serving bowl* in *fridge*. You'll need to microwave the CHILI for **2 minutes per dinner bowl** on date night.

If making the night of the date, set timer for **5 minutes** to let CHILI cool.

1. Grab BAG of MICROWAVABLE RICE. Open sides of top as instructed. Put BAG in microwave and cook for 90 seconds.
2. When RICE is done, remove bag and tear off top. Be careful, this mofo is hot! Let cool.
3. Add TOMATOES to salad bowls.
4. Pour RICE into serving bowl #1.
5. Add 3 Handfuls of CHEDDAR CHEESE to serving bowl #2.
6. Ask Ms. Right Now if she prefers TORTILLAS or OYSTER CRACKERS with her chili.
7. Pour TORTILLA CHIPS or OYSTER CRACKERS onto a plate.
8. Add SALAD DRESSING to SALADS.
9. Measure ½ Cup of SOUR CREAM and add to serving bowl #3.
10. When oven timer goes off, spoon CHILI into two bowls.
11. Carry SALADS and CHEESE and SOUR CREAM bowls to table.
12. Carry out dinner plates.
13. Dinner is served.

Brent's Veggie Pasta

This is the second of two recipes Brent Pickett has contributed to Bachelor 101. If you haven't tried his Shrimp Scampi , you are missing out.

These meals made me wonder why he didn't get laid more when he was single. So I asked him. Brent explained he was "waiting for a special woman to cook for, someone like my wife." Wow. This guy is good.

Ease: 2 Chefs
Cost: $41
Preparation Time: 10 minutes
Cooking Time: 40 minutes (including time to boil the water)

Ingredients:
Angel Hair Pasta – 1 sixteen-ounce Box; $2.55
Extra Virgin Olive Oil – 2 Tablespoons; $6-13 per bottle
Roma Tomatoes – 6 of them; $4.50 per pound
Fresh Basil - $2.99 (*You get screwed on basil b/c you'll only use, like, ¼ of it and end up throwing out the rest*)
Shredded Mozzarella Cheese – 2 Cups; $3.39 per 16-ounce bag
Sea Salt – 2 Teaspoons; $1.29 per shaker
Pre-Washed Mixed Salad – 1 Bag; $5
Salad Dressing – Bottle of your choice; $2
Take-n-Bake Bread – 1 Loaf; $2.00 (Found in Bakery section of supermarket)
Butter – 1 Stick; $5.50 per package

Wine Recommendation: Pinot Noir or, if feeling adventurous, Pinotage

Tools, etc:
Small Bowl
Large Serving Bowl
Large Pasta Pot
Measuring Spoons
Oven Mitts
Wooden Spoon
Colander (the thingy with all the holes; it's for draining pasta)
Stopwatch

Directions:

1. 30 minutes before you want to eat, add WATER to pasta pot (add the amount listed in the pasta box's directions). Cover pot. Crank up heat.

2. Place colander in sink.

3. Place 1 stick of BUTTER on a small plate. (You won't be cooking with it. This is just a move to make sure Ms. Right Now doesn't tear her bread apart later due to the butter being freezing cold.)

4. Wash TOMATOES. Place tomatoes in colander to dry.

5. Chop 10 sprigs of BASIL. Add to small bowl.
6. On the cutting board chop TOMATOES. Throw out TOPS and BOTTOMS of TOMATOES.
7. Run WATER in sink. Rinse off icky, green SEEDS from TOMATOES.
8. Add TOMATOES to small bowl.
9. Rinse out colander and leave it in the sink.
10. Pre-heat oven to 400 degrees.
11. Measure 2 Cups OF MOZARELLA CHEESE. Set aside.
12. When WATER boils, add ANGLE HAIR PASTA to pot.
13. Add 6 shakes of SEA SALT to water. Cover pot.
14. Set stopwatch for time listed on PASTA BOX.
15. Open TAKE-N-BAKE BREAD.
16. Put on oven mitt. Open oven door. Slide out oven rack.
17. Place BREAD on rack. Slide in rack. Close door. Take off mitt.
18. Set oven timer for time listed on TAKE-N-BAKE BREAD BAG.
19. Open BAG OF SALAD. Add to salad bowls.
20. Measure 1 TEAspoon of SEA SALT and add to large serving bowl.
21. When stopwatch goes off, turn off flame under pasta pot.
22. Put on oven mitt.
23. Carry pot to sink.
24. Pour WATER and PASTA into colander. Let drain.
25. Once the WATER has stopped dripping from the colander, pour PASTA into the large serving bowl.
26. Measure 2 TABLEspoons of OLIVE OIL and pour over PASTA.
27. When oven timer goes off, turn off oven.
28. Put on oven mitt. Open oven door. Slide out bottom rack.
29. Remove BREAD and place on cutting board.
30. Slide in rack. Close oven door. Take off oven mitt.
31. Add BASIL and TOMATOES to pasta.
32. This is where things get tricky, dude. So pay attention! Don't dump all of the cheese in at once because the hot pasta will melt the cheese into a big clump. That's no bueno. You want it mixed evenly throughout.
33. In measuring cup, measure ½ CUP of MOZARELLA CHEESE.
34. Use your fingers to sprinkle CHEESE all over pasta.

35. Use wooden spoon to mix CHEESE and PASTA.
36. Repeat steps 33 – 34.
37. Repeat mixing with the wooden spoon.
38. Repeat steps 33 – 34.
39. Repeat mixing.
40. Repeat steps 33 – 34 for final time.
41. Measure 1 TEAspoon of SEA SALT and add to pasta.
42. Repeat mixing. You are all done with the pasta.
43. Slice ¼ loaf of bread and place two slices on dinner plates.
44. Add SALAD DRESSING to salad bowls.
45. Put the PASTA onto dinner plates.
46. Carry butter plate and salad bowls out to table.
47. Carry dinner plates to table.
48. Dinner is served!

VEGGIE SIDES

As I pointed out in the introductory chapter, salad is a perfectly acceptable vegetable offering. Actually <u>cooking</u> a vegetable may spell disaster by creating a four-car pileup on your stovetop. But if you feel some irresistible need to make an extra veggie, these two are fairly simple.

Kayce's Raspberry Vinaigrette Asparagus

Kayce Seamster is the daughter of Curt Croom, my old boss and famed inventor of "Curt's Crumby Chicken." I met her when I was 24 and she was on summer break from college. I'll let your imagination run wild.

Alas, I never checked the box on that whole "Boss's daughter" fantasy. But I got this awesome recipe! So I got that going for me. Which is nice.

Important Note: Asparagus makes some people's pee smell funny. This is due to the manner in which our digestive system breaks down a sulfur compound called mercaptan. Not all humans have the gene for the enzyme that breaks down mercaptan, so those weirdos (can you tell I have the gene?) don't notice any aromatic difference. This info makes for a fun conversation starter in a pinch.

Ease: 1 Chef
Cost: $5
Preparation Time: 5 minutes
Cooking Time: 15 minutes

Ingredients:
Asparagus – 10; $3.05 per bunch
Ken's Raspberry Vinegarette Salad Dressing – 2 TABLEspoons; $2.00 per bottle

Tools, etc:
Measuring Cup
Paring Knife
Cutting Board
Large Saucepot
Oven Mitt
Colander (the plastic thingy with the holes in it)
Serving Dish
Measuring Spoons

Directions:
1. Measure 4 Cups of WATER and add to large saucepot.
2. Put large saucepot on stovetop burner. Cover saucepot.

3. Turn on flame under saucepan and crank to high.
4. Wash ASAPARAGUS.
5. On cutting board, chop off 1 inch from the bottoms of ASPARAGUS.
6. Throw out BOTTOMS of ASAPARAGUS.
7. Put colander in sink.
8. When WATER boils, add ASPARAGUS to large saucepot.
9. Set oven timer for 4 minutes.
10. When oven timer goes off, turn off flame under large saucepot.
11. Put on oven mitt.
12. Carry large saucepot to sink.
13. Dump ASPARAGUS into colander. Let drain.
14. Return saucepan to stovetop burner. Take off oven mitt.
15. Rinse ASPARAGUS with COLD WATER for 20 seconds.
16. Put serving dish next to sink.
17. Add ASPARAGUS to serving dish.
18. Measure 2 TEAspoons of RASPEBERRY VINEGARETTE DRESSING and pour all over ASPARAGUS.
19. Place in refrigerator until dinnertime.
20. When dinner is ready, add CHILLED ASPARAGUS to dinner plates.
21. Your veggie is served!

Gretchen's Lemon-Basil Carrots

Gretchen Baker made a big mistake in 1993; she married Curt Croom. That would be Curt of "Curt's Crumby Chicken" fame. Had she not wed him, she never would've met me. It's the little decisions that haunt you, right?

Gretchen saved me from starving in Japan, inviting me over weekly for a scrumptious dinner. My boss did not share her enthusiasm, but she ruled the roost. You go, G-Meister!

Gretchen's sister Donna Franklin contributed to "Three Person's Chicken Divan" fame.

Ease: 2 Chefs
Cost: $25
Preparation Time: 3 minutes
Cooking Time: 15 minutes

Ingredients:
Baby Carrots – 20; $5 per one-pound bag
Butter – 1 TABLEspoon; $5.50 per package of 4 sticks

Lemon Juice – 2 TEAspoons; $2 per bottle
Dried Basil Flakes – $4.39 per bottle
Garlic Salt – 2; $2.99 per bottle
Black Pepper – 1 shake; $2.19 per bottle

Tools, etc:
Paring Knife
Cutting Board
Small Saucepan
Colander (The thingy with all the holes; it's for draining stuff in the sink)
Oven Mitt
Measuring Spoons
Wooden Spoon

Directions:

1. Wash BABY CARROTS.
2. On cutting board, slice CARROTS into 1.5 inches slices.
3. Place SLICED CARROTS into small saucepan.
4. Fill saucepan with just enough WATER to cover SLICED CARROTS.
5. Place small saucepan on stovetop burner.
6. Turn on flame under saucepan to medium.
7. Set oven timer for 10 minutes.
8. Place colander in sink.
9. Cut 1 TABLEspoon of BUTTER (Use the ruler on the wax paper wrapper to measure this). Set BUTTER aside for later.
10. When oven timer goes off, turn off flame under saucepan.
11. Put on oven mitt.
12. Carry saucepan to sink.
13. Dump CARROTS and WATER into colander. Let drain.
14. Dump SLICED CARROTS back into saucepan.
15. Return saucepan to stovetop burner.
16. Add TABLEspoon of BUTTER to saucepan.
17. Measure 1 TEAspoon of DRIED BASIL FLAKES and add to saucepan.
18. Measure 1/8 TEAspoon of GARLIC SALT and add to saucepan.
19. Measure 2 TEAspoons of LEMON JUICE and add to saucepan.
20. Grab BLACK PEPPER and shake 1 time above saucepan.
21. Turn on flame below saucepan to low.
22. Watch saucepan to see when BUTTER melts.

23. When BUTTER melts, turn off flame.
24. Use wooden spoon to stir SLICED CARROTS and SAUCE.
25. Add SLICED CARROTS to dinner plates. Be sure to scoop extra SAUCE on CARROTS.
26. Your veggie is served!

STARCHY SIDES

Again, microwavable rice is a perfectly acceptable starch offering.

Curt's Baked Potatoes in The Microwave

Yes, that is an oxymoron.

Curt Croom has helped you out yet again. If you absolutely *have to have* baked potatoes with your meatloaf, this is the recipe for you.

Ease: 1 Chef
Cost: $10
Preparation Time: 3 minutes
Cooking Time: 15 minutes

Ingredients:
Russet (Baked) Potatoes – 4; $4.00 ($1 each)
Butter – 4 TABLEspoons; $5.50 per package of 4 sticks

Tools, etc:
Scrubbing Sponge (the kind with the Astroturf on the one side)
Paper Towels
Large Plate
Small Plate
Paring Knife
Fork

Directions:

1. 25 minutes before you want to eat, scrub POTATOES with Astroturf sponge.
2. Pat dry with a paper towel.
3. Place 4 POTATOES on large plate.
4. Take fork and puncture each POTATO in 10 different places.
5. Place large plate in microwave.
6. Set microwave timer for 20 minutes. (Note: If you were only microwaving 1 POTATO, you'd cook it for 11 minutes. When you microwave additional potatoes, add 3 minutes for each one.)
7. Cut 4 TABLEspoons of BUTTER (Use the ruler on the wax paper wrapper to measure the amount).
8. Put BUTTER on small plate for later.

9. When microwave stops, take out large plate.
10. Cut open 1 POTATO to make sure it's done.
11. If done, add 1 POTATO to each dinner plate.
12. If the potato is not done after 20 minutes, return large plate to microwave for 3 minutes of cooking.
13. Your "baked" potatoes are served!

Poeppe's Party Potatoes

Michelle (Poeppe) Egan is married to my old roomie Steve, of "Easy Pork" fame.

The Grandmaster Shelley Shel is a very forgiving woman; I once commented positively on her "dishwater blonde" hair. I quickly learned that that is not a compliment. I meant to say, "Strawberry blonde".

I made this recipe for an Easter 2008 potluck dinner…voted #1 dish!

Ease: 2 Chefs
Preparation Time: 90 minutes (70 of which are defrosting the frozen potatoes)
Cooking Time: 50 minutes
Cost: $27

Ingredients:
Frozen Hash Browns – 1 two-pound bag; $2.50 (*You may only find a 30-ounce bag. I spent five minutes searching in vain for a two-pound bag. Don't waste your time; people won't miss the extra two ounces!*)
Butter – ¾ Cup melted and "divided"; $5.50 for package of 4 sticks (*"Divided" means, "Portions of it will be used at different times during the process."*)
Sea Salt – 1 TABLEspoon; $3.99 per bottle
Black Pepper – 1 TABLEspoon; $1.29
Brown Onion – ½ Cup Chopped; 89 cents per pound (takes less than 1 Onion)
Cream of Chicken soup – 1 Can; $1.39
Sour Cream – 1 Pint; 2.69 (1 pint = 16-ounces)
Mild Cheddar Cheese – 2 Cups Shredded; $2.50 per 8-ounce bag
Corn Flakes – 2 Cups (crushed); $3.89 per small box

Tools, etc:
Colander (The thingy with all the holes; it's for draining stuff in the sink)
Chef's Knife
Cutting Board
Large Mixing Bowl
Measuring Cup
Measuring Spoons
Small Plate
Wooden Spoon
Large Baking Dish
Ziploc Bag

Small Mixing Bowl
Oven Mitt – 2
Dinner Spoon
Spatula

Instructions:
1. One hour prior to cooking, place BAG of HASH BROWNS on counter to defrost.
2. What's that? You screwed up #1 and failed to let the HASH BROWNS defrost? No worries, I did the same thing. You can still rally and get the job done by following steps 3 – 9. If you were a GOOD BOY and followed the directions, happily skip to step 10.
3. Place 1/3 of the HASH BROWNS on a large plate.
4. Place large plate in microwave and use the auto-defrost mode.
5. Place colander in sink.
6. When microwave finishes, dump HASH BROWNS into colander.
7. Using your fist, push down on HASH BROWNS to squeeze the WATER out of them.
8. When WATER has been removed, add HASH BROWNS to large mixing bowl.
9. Repeat steps 3 – 8 for next 1/3 of FROZEN HASH BROWNS.
10. Repeat steps 3 – 8 for final 1/3 of FROZEN HASH BROWNS.
11. Place colander in sink.
12. Open one small corner of HASH BROWNS BAG.
13. Stand in front of sink.
14. Squeeze out WATER from HASH BROWNS over colander.
15. Dump HASH BROWNS into colander.
16. Set oven timer for 5 minutes to make sure HASH BROWNS drained.
17. When oven timer goes off, add DEFROSTED HASH BROWNS to large mixing bowl.
18. Pre-heat oven to 350 degrees.
19. If you don't want to cry while chopping ONIONS, take a dinner spoon and suck on it. Seriously.
20. On a cutting board, chop off both ends of the ONION. Then, cut the REMAINDER in half.
21. Remove SKIN and throw the skin in the trash.
22. You now have a halved onion that has been cut on two sides. You'll only be using one half of the onion, so you can save the other half or chuck it.
23. Turn ONION so that 1 cut side faces you. Choose 1 UNCUT SIDE.
24. Thinly slice along that uncut side until the whole thing is sliced. The point here is to slice the onion as thinly as possible. Think of it like a wet t-shirt contest, only instead of "Skin to Win!" this motto is, "Thin to Win!"

25. Chop ONION into ¼" x ¼" pieces, i.e. the size of the onions on a McDonald's hamburger.
26. Fill measuring cup with ONION until you have ½ Cup of CHOPPED ONIONS.
27. Add ½ Cup of CHOPPED ONIONS to large mixing bowl.
28. Use your fingers to evenly spread out the ONION in the large mixing bowl.
29. Furiously scrub hands with DISH SOAP. ONION will stink up your cuticles, which won't go over well later when you try to feed her dessert.
30. Measure 1 TABLEspoon of SEA SALT and add to large mixing bowl.
31. Measure 1 TABLEspoon of PEPPER and add to large mixing bowl.
32. Cut ¼ Cup of BUTTER (Use the ruler on the wax paper wrapper to measure this) and put BUTTER on small plate.
33. Place small plate in microwave. Heat for 30 seconds. If this fails to melt the BUTTER, then nuke it again for 10 more seconds.
34. Add 1 Can of CREAM OF CHICKEN SOUP to large mixing bowl.
35. Add 1 Pint of SOUR CREAM to large mixing bowl.
36. Spread 2 Cups of SHREDDED CHEDDAR CHEESE all around the large mixing bowl.
37. Pour ¼ Cup of MELTED BUTTER all around the large mixing bowl.
38. Using wooden spoon, thoroughly mix EVERYTHING in large mixing bowl.
39. Scoop MIXTURE into large baking dish.
40. Cut ½ Cup of BUTTER (Use the ruler on the wax paper wrapper to measure this) and put BUTTER on small plate.
41. Place small plate in microwave. Heat for 60 seconds. If this fails to melt the BUTTER, then nuke it again for 10 more seconds.
42. Pour 2 Cups of CORN FLAKES into Ziploc bag and seal bag.
43. Crush the shit out of those FLAKES.
44. Pour CRUSHED FLAKES into small mixing bowl.
45. Pour ½ Cup of MELTED BUTTER into small mixing bowl.
46. Mix stuff in small mixing bowl.
47. Pour BUTTERED FLAKES evenly on top of POTATO MIXTURE in large baking dish. This may be tough to do, so use a dinner spoon to scrape the "sauce" onto bare areas.
48. Put on oven mitts. Open oven door. Slide out rack.
49. Place large baking dish on rack. Slide in rack. Close oven. Take off mitts.
50. Set oven timer for 50 minutes.
51. When oven timer goes off, turn off oven.
52. Put on oven mitts. Open oven door. Slide out rack.

53. Remove large baking dish and place on stovetop burners to cool.
54. Slide in rack. Close oven. Take off mitts.
55. Use spatula to cut and add POEPPE PARTY POTATOES to dinner plates.
56. The side dish is served!

DESSERT

Dessert

No hard work here, brother.

For me, there are two options: ICE CREAM from the supermarket or CHOCOLATE CHIP COOKIES from a bakery.

If you wanna get crazy with the ice cream, buy hot fudge and whipped cream. Who knows what wild thoughts the latter will inspire in Ms. Right Now…

BREAKFAST

a.k.a. "May You Be So Lucky!"

Jimmy O's Breakfast Burrito

You wish you had it as good as Jim Ortiz.

Wouldn't it be cool to tell people you took a two-year break from Harvard to play poker professionally? Wouldn't you like to mention that you spend half the year in Rio de Janeiro training with the guys who invented Brazilian Jiu-Jitsu? Wouldn't it be fun to retire at 38?

Jimmy stressed that this recipe works best for one guy and <u>two</u> women. Godspeed on making that happen!

The nice thing about this meal is you simply use whatever you have left over in the fridge: veggies, cheese and meat from previous night's dinner.

Here is an important tip to ensure you don't overcook the eggs: if you think your eggs look done in the pan, they <u>will be overdone</u> on the plate.

So, make sure you turn off the flame under the eggs when they still look moist. You can move the frying pan to a cool burner and the eggs will continue to cook.

Feel free to rock out the mimosas or Bloody Mary's!

Ease: 3 Chefs
Cost: $44
Preparation Time: 10 minutes
Cooking Time: 5 minutes

Ingredients:
Eggs – 6; $2.50 per dozen
Milk – 1 TABLEspoon per egg; $1.79 per quart
Extra Virgin Olive Oil – 2 TABLEspoons; $6-13
Shredded Pepper Jack Cheese – ½ Cup; $5.29 per bag
Sea Salt – ¼ TEAspoon; $3.99 per jar
Cracked Black Pepper – ½ TEAspoon; $2.19 per bottle
Garlic Powder – ¼ TEAspoon; $6.29
Large Wheat Tortillas – 6; $2.00
Salsa – however much you want; $3.00
Avocado – 2; $1.99 each
Orange Juice – ½ Gallon; $4

Tools, etc:
Mixing Bowl
Paring Knife
Cutting Board

Measuring Cup
Measuring Spoons
Fork
Large non-stick Frying Pan (*If you are only making breakfast for yourself, i.e. 2-3 EGGS, then use a smaller pan. It's important to not let the EGG MIXTURE run too thin, as it will not become fluffy the way most people like it.*)
Spatula
Frying Pan
Large Plate
Dish Towel
Small Plate
Bowl

Directions:

1. Wash VEGETABLES. Dry them with paper towels.
2. On cutting board, chop VEGGIES into slices ½ inch thick.
3. Place large non-stick frying pan on stovetop burner.
4. Measure 2 TABLEspoons of OLIVE OIL and add to large non-stick frying pan.
5. Crank up FLAME to high under large non-stick frying pan.
6. Add VEGETABLES to large non-stick frying pan.
7. Set oven timer for 3 minutes.
8. Place mixing bowl on countertop next to sink.
9. Crack an EGG and add to mixing bowl. Throw out EGG SHELL.
10. Repeat step 4 for each of the remaining EGGS.
11. Stir VEGETABLES so they don't burn.
12. Measure ¼ Cup of MILK and add to mixing bowl.
13. Measure ¼ TEAspoon of SEA SALT and add to large non-stick frying pan.
14. Measure ½ TEAspoon of BLACK PEPPER and add to large non-stick frying pan.
15. Use fork to whisk EGG MIXTURE. "Whisking" basically means stirring rapidly in shallow circles; but it's not your normal vertical stirring (like mixing a can of paint), but a horizontal stirring.
16. Mix well until the color and texture are uniform throughout.
17. When oven timer goes off, pour EGG MIXTURE into large non-stick frying pan.
18. Reduce FLAME to low.
19. Tilt frying pan in every direction to cover bottom of pan with MIXTURE.
20. Return non-stick frying pan to stovetop burner.
21. Set oven timer for 1 minute. Don't do anything to the EGGS! You will see the mixture solidify.

22. Measure ¼ TEAspoon of GARLIC POWDER and sprinkle throughout MIXTURE in large non-stick frying pan.
23. Measure ½ Cup of PEPPER JACK CHEESE and sprinkle throughout MIXTURE in large non-stick frying pan.
24. When oven timer goes off, slide spatula under EDGE of COOKED EGGS.
25. Use spatula to lift EDGES and fold them into the center of the frying pan.
26. Use spatula to flip EGGS over so that what was once on bottom is now on top.
27. You do not want to let the EGGS turn brown.
28. Continue scraping, lifting and folding. Bottom to top, bottom to top.
29. Use spatula to chop up EGGS. Bigger pieces are fluffier; smaller ones are drier.
30. Turn off flame under EGGS and move non-stick frying pan to a cool stovetop burner.
31. Place second frying pan on another stovetop burner.
32. Set FLAME under second frying pan to low.
33. Place 1 TORTILLA in second frying pan to warm it. After 20 seconds, flip TORTILLA.
34. After 20 seconds, remove TORTILLA from pan and place on large plate.
35. Cover TORTILLA on large plate with dish towel to keep warm.
36. Repeat steps 34 – 35 for remaining TORTILLAS.
37. Spoon half the EGGS onto each breakfast plate.
38. Slice AVOCADO in half. Slice 8 pieces and place them on small plate.
39. Pour half SALSA into bowl.
40. Pour ORANGE JUICE. Carry glasses to table.
41. Carry avocado plate and salsa bowl to table.
42. Carry tortilla plate and breakfast plates to table.
43. Breakfast is served!

PART TWO: ABODE

GETTING STARTED

Pardon the vacuuming pun, but cleaning sucks. There's really no getting around that fact. Unfortunately, there's no avoiding the fact that you have to clean your place if you want Ms. Right Now to make herself comfortable.

I think half the turn-on of the French Maid fantasy is simply that she might tidy up afterwards.

Here's a good way to approach cleaning, taken from our Elder Statesman of Modernism, Homer Simpson. Homer's ghost is panicked that he won't be able to get into Heaven, and he asks Marge for suggestions on how best to do it.

Marge: Well, I got a whole list of chores: clean the garage, paint the house...

Homer's ghost: Whoa, whoa, whoa. I'm just trying to get in; I'm not running for Jesus!

Boys… we are also trying to get into Heaven, in a manner of speaking. And, like Marge says, chores are required.

CLEANING ESSENTIALS

- Vacuum
- Swiffer w/ Swiffer pads (This does a killer job of cleaning bare floors)
- Wet Swiffer w/ wet Swiffer pads (washes bare floors)
- Paper Towels
- Rags
- Bathroom Cleaning Spray (Comet, Lysol, etc.)
- Glass Cleaner (Glass Plus, Windex, etc.)
- Q-Tips
- Brillo pads
- Old Sponge w/ green Astroturf side – 2
- Toilet Brush
- Toilet Brush Holder
- Baking Soda
- New Sponge w/ green Astroturf side
- Stick-Up air freshener
- Carpet Fresh
- Febreze Anti-microbial Fabric Freshener
- Magazine Rack

ON THE WAY IN

Needs: Swiffer and dry Swiffer towels, or vacuum with hose attachment

Start at the start. Outside your building or house.

Pick up and throw out all the ancient Pennysavers, unsolicited restaurant menus and "Have You Seen Me?" missing person postcards.

If she has to climb an indoor staircase en route to your apartment, you need to make sure the first thing she sees doesn't repulse her. In that spirit, it's a good idea to get rid of the cobwebs, pebbles, and dried mud that can accumulate in the corners of each step. On carpet or bare floor, you can use the vacuum with hose. The Swiffer (once you've attached a dry towel) only works on the bare floor.

The Swiffer is a contradiction in terms – a fun utensil for cleaning. I don't understand the physics behind it, but somehow all the dirt and hair clings to the dry towel (to maximize each towel, take it off above the garbage can, so that the crap doesn't fall onto the floor; flip over the dry towel and reuse the bottom side). All you have to do is move the Swiffer forward and back, left and right, like a metal detector guy at the beach.

Outside your apartment door. While not encouraging you to break any laws, it might behoove you to "temporarily" take down the Police Tape and the eviction notice.

Do you have a Welcome Mat? If so and it's less than two years old, that's good. If it's older, chuck that bad boy. You can buy a decent one at Target for $10. While you're looking down there – on the floor, not at Target – check for more spare dirt, etc. Swiffer/vacuum away whatever you find.

Once inside your apartment, make sure there is no footwear (especially not "aromatic" running shoes) sitting by the door. Unless you're operating Asian style, that is, with a "no shoes in the house" rule; then it's perfectly acceptable to have them neatly arranged door side. But not the running shoes!

Speaking of shoes, how long since you had yours shined? If time permits, drop them off at the local shoe shine guy; most full-service car washes have one. If you don't have the time, go get your shine box, Tommy. Or, at the very least, grab a wet rag and wipe down the pair you're going to wear on the date. Clean and dull is better than dirty and dull. My Opa – that's German for grandpa – always told me, "You can tell everything about a man by his shoes." What if her grandfather told her the same thing??? No need to risk it.

Harvard grads, since you already mentioned your alma mater within ten seconds of meeting her, anyway, you don't need to hang your diploma next to the coat rack.

Lastly, you need to recon your "spot." We've all got one – that special place where we drop our keys, wallet, cell phone, loose change, stripper's business cards, etc. Wherever it is, give your spot a thorough once-over. Who knows what is sitting out in plain sight for her to discover? Move any incriminating evidence to the secret location where you'll be storing your porn and other "sensitive" items.

KITCHEN

Needs: New sponge with scrubbing side, Glass Plus, paper towels, Swiffer, Wet Swiffer, Arm & Hammer baking soda, cereal bowl, candles.

Did you know that the military acronym "K.P." stands for Kitchen Patrol?

This isn't a chapter on how to keep the kitchen clean while cooking your masterpiece. She won't care if the sink is full and the stove and counters are a huge mess. In fact, that will serve as evidence that you actually made the meal, rather than surreptitiously ordering out (I know the thought has crossed your mind). So, go crazy when cooking.

This is a guide for the pre-game preparation of the kitchen. One rule of life holds that, no matter how sweet the rest of the home, more people hang out in the kitchen during a party. Same could be true on your date; especially if there are still a bunch of things you need to do meal-wise. And, if you plan on sharing the chopping and dicing – which many women consider romantic <u>and</u> gives you dozens of opportunities for "accidental" contact – then you need to have the kitchen looking good, soldier.

When painting a room, you wouldn't do the walls before you did the ceiling, because that would cause specks of paint to splat down on the freshly done walls. You would start with the ceiling, and then do the walls. Cleaning a room is similar to painting – start high and work your way down.

Take a look in the four corners of the room: see any arachnid apartment complexes? They need to be razed. A big, scary spider is all right, as it'll provide you with the opportunity to heroically save the damsel in distress. Spider webs, however, only prove that you're harboring terrorists. And Pakistan isn't getting laid.

Grab the vacuum hose, and suck down those webs.

Now, on to the refrigerator.

Remove everything from the outside of the fridge and freezer doors. Soak the doors with Glass Plus, paying close attention to the area around the handles, just like in one of those TV commercials. Wipe the doors down with a couple of paper towels.

Take a deep breath…and rip open the refrigerator door. You are now in "Purge Mode."

Throw out anything you don't immediately remember buying, won't pass the whiff test or has condensation inside the bottle.

Unless you personally opened them yesterday, toss <u>all</u> jars of salsa.

Check the cold cuts and veggies drawers; you don't want her finding surprises later.

Now, carry those drawers over to the sink and scald them with the hottest water your faucet has to offer.

Wet the sponge. Wipe down all the shelves and racks in the fridge, making sure they are completely unstained.

Open the box of Arm & Hammer and place it in the back of the fridge. Yes, I know every Grandma in the world does this. That's because baking soda absorbs odors, sonny. Close the door.

Open the freezer door. Make sure there are no reminders of the warm Coke can you put in there last fall "just for, like, ten minutes, only to get it cold." You know, the one you discovered a week later. If you find Slurpee parts, wipe them up with the sponge.

Empty out your ice trays in the sink, and make fresh ones. Yes, ice can go bad.

Here's an unrelated but fabulous rule for life: my dad says you should always bring two bags of ice or two folding chairs to a party, because the host can never have too much of either. Rich Reidy – the guy should've been on a Miller Lite "Man Law" commercial.

Ah, alcohol. Right now, drop everything!

Put the chardonnay, beer, tonic and club soda in the fridge and the vodka in the freezer. As long as the drinks are done correctly, you can atone for any meal malady.

If you are a frosted mug guy, make that happen.

If you want to make a classy impression, have a bottle of champagne chilling in the fridge at all times. You probably don't want to offer it right away – that might seem a bit much to her – but if things go well, she might like a taste of bubbly with/after dessert. And, even if you don't open it up, Ms. Right Now will see that you're a guy who always has champagne handy; nobody ever lost points for that.

Back to the fridge doors.

Now that they're clean, you need to think about what you want decorating them. Just as the kitchen serves as the nucleus of the apartment, the refrigerator serves as the center of the kitchen.

She will make a beeline to read whatever is on your fridge, so be careful not to post anything negative – six parking tickets, angry statements from creditors, etc. Magnets from restaurants, sports teams and tourist locales are fine; magnets from bail bondsmen are not.

The easiest, safest and most effective way to spruce up your refrigerator is with kids' artwork. If any nieces or nephews live locally, call their mother and tell her you need some drawings addressed to "Uncle" ASAP. If time doesn't permit it, make a mental note to do so at the next earliest opportunity. Chicks love guys who aren't too macho to display their love for children; what better way to do this than by displaying the terrible artwork of little people? It doesn't have to be drawn by relatives, though; any child will do. In fact, kids of friends may actually be better, because you'll score more points thanks to the lack of a family obligation to hang it on the freezer.

From cold to hot. The microwave.

I'm guessing you haven't cleaned it since ever.

First, fill up the cereal bowl with water, put it inside and cook it for a minute. The steam created will help loosen the splatter of a million nukings. Open the door carefully, so exploding water doesn't blind you, like in that Internet myth.

Grab the sponge and scrub like crazy. Take out the glass circle that spins in the middle and wash it in the sink. Don't forget to put it back after it's dry.

Wash the inside of the door. Then, close said door and grab the Glass Plus. Spray the door and wipe it down with a paper towel.

Move over to the sink. Hopefully, you have a dishwasher, but most bachelors are not so lucky.

You gotta do the dishes and put them away in the cabinets *before* she arrives. Seriously. Throw the wine glasses in, too. I don't care if you think they're clean. They're not. Trust me: dust affects the bouquet. If you don't own wine glasses, you need to get some. Only four, and you can get them at Target, Crate and Barrel (not Creighton Barrel, which is what I thought till I was 25), or Williams Sonoma. Or from a female neighbor; this'll let her know you like to cook and that you have a social life.

Hold on. You're not done at the sink, yet.

If you have a dish rack for drying, you probably have one of those angled rubber mats, too. I can see the dirt and grime from here. Pick up the rack, and wipe down the rubber. Replace rack.

Sinks are nearly always located in front of a window, making them great locations for a – gasp – plant. I'm not talking major shrubbery here, just one of those green, vine-like things that are impossible to kill.

Hang the plant from the ceiling. A single guy with living things in his home (not to be confused with mold, mice, ants, etc.) is a guy not totally terrified of one day entertaining the thought of maybe having children. She'll dig it.

On the topic of living creatures, obviously owning a dog is a huge plus in numerous areas. A cat accomplishes the same goals, while adding two possibly unwanted ones: triggering her allergies and proving you're gay.

Regardless, make sure that the food and water bowls are cleaner than everything in the house, including the wineglasses. Rover's bed shouldn't be covered with hair or smell like a dog sleeps there. Speaking of smelling, if you have time to give Rover a bath, do so.

Lastly, look for animal hair that has collected all along the baseboards. I will not even get into litter box maintenance.

Where's your trash?

Walk over there. If you do not have a <u>clearly designated</u> recyclables bin, you need to make one. Even a Recyclables Bag will do the trick. *Green…is good.* Women think ecofriendliness is hot. ABR – Always Be Recycling!

However, you should not have three cases of empties inside the bin, lest she think you're a guy who sits around and pounds beers with his roomies on a Tuesday night while playing X-Box.

Remember to actually use the recyclables bin when cleaning up after dinner.

Since I don't know if you'll be dining in the kitchen, dining room or living room, I'll cover how to set the table in this section.

Obviously, you need to set two places. Across from one another is better for a date early in the relationship for two reasons: one, you won't freak her out with the creepy proximity; two, you get to make natural eye contact throughout dinner. If you're one of those guys who avoid eye contact, then, by all means, put the place settings on either side of the table corner.

Place a candle in the middle of the table. The dinner plate goes one inch from the table edge. The *fork* goes to the left of the plate, the *knife* to the right of the plate (blade inwards), and the *spoon* to the right of the knife. If you're serving salad, you need to do two extra things: place another fork next to his brother to the left of the plate and place the salad bowl on top of the plate.

The bread plate belongs on the upper left, while wine and water glasses go on the upper right. How do I know that?

Hold up each of your hands. Now, make the "A.O.K." sign with each. Your right hand looks like the letter "d" and your left looks like the letter "b", correct? D is for drinks and B is for bread. Drinks on the right, bread on the left. I learned that trick at a friend's bachelor party in Vegas. And wives say nothing constructive happens on those weekends!

You should use cloth napkins (For real. You can get them at any of the aforementioned stores) but the nice paper kind will suffice in a jam. You don't, however, need to use placemats, since no self-respecting single guy owns placemats. *Unless*, of course, the placemats have been made at kindergarten by your five-year old niece. Serve from the left side, clear the table from the right.

You probably haven't given any consideration to the chairs, but they're undoubtedly dusty: on top and between any spokes that run from the top to the base.

Wipe off those areas. You'll be amazed how dirty the rag gets.

On to the kitchen floor. Why? Because if all goes well you might end up *on* the kitchen floor post-meal!

Grab your Swiffer and pick up all the crumbs, dirt, etc. Next, wield your Wet Swiffer and make that floor shine! Throw out the dirty pads for both Swiffers.

One last thing: hang a clean hand towel near the sink. After dinner, Ms. Right Now should – if her momma raised her right – offer to help do the dishes. This is a perfect time for some relaxed banter and lots of accidental touching.

Now, your kitchen looks and smells great. Nice work.

Hide a condom someplace handy, just in case. Actually, don't. That'd be a tough one to explain to her.

LIVING ROOM

Needs: damp rag, paper towels, candles, magazine rack, Glass Plus, vacuum, Swiffer, Wet Swiffer, Stick-Up air freshener, Carpet Fresh, Febreze Anti-microbial Fabric Freshener, one quarter (25-cent piece)

No pressure or anything, but this might be the most important room in the house. After all, you and she will probably be spending a lot of the date in here. No worries, mate; there are lots of easy fixes in the living room.

Again, start high. Grab the vacuum hose, and suck down those webs.

Next, turn off the ceiling fan and carefully look up at the blades once they've stopped moving. See the layer of gray-brown fur hanging over the edges of each one? That isn't a strip of soundproofing that came with the fan.

Either climb on a chair and wipe down the blades with the wet rag, or use the vacuum's hose to clean them off.

Take a look at the "art work" adorning your walls. Neon beer signs are acceptable; beer posters with bikini-clad chicks are not.

Got any framed photos of your family, or at least your mother? Better get some before she starts thinking you're a serial killer. Several of the women surveyed, however, cautioned against having too many pictures of Mom – they make you look like a mama's boy, at best, and a boy who likes boys, at worst.

Shots of a family pet are guaranteed to induce an "Awww." Pictures of your ex do not. The girls also complained about those annoying framed prints that your boss has on the wall of his office, the ones with the cheesy inspirational messages. So you might want to 86 any of those.

Take the damp rag and wipe down the tops and edges of anything hanging on the walls.

If you just wiped down a gun rack with actual guns in it…that's probably a deal breaker in Blue States. Even in a Red State, unless you know for sure that you're dating a direct descendant of Annie Oakley's, odds are she will spot your arsenal, click her spurs three times and disappear before you serve the appetizer. Consider yourself warned, Tex. Ditto for antlers or anything that ever required a conversation with a taxidermist.

Speaking of spooking her, reptiles are not conducive to getting naked. This is not up for discussion.

Next, take the rag and wipe it along the edges of your halogen lamps (c'mon, everybody's got at least one). Try not to cough on the dust you've kicked up.

Next, move to the bookcase (I hope I'm not going out on a limb, here, by assuming that you read books) and give the shelves a quick wipe down with the rag.

If you have any books published since you did your required summer reading, put those on a shelf that's right at your girl's line of sight. "I Know This Much Is True" and "Cold Mountain" will demonstrate your sensitive side, while anything by Malcolm Gladwell's will let her know you're hip to smart non-fiction. If you have that book about bees and their secrets…she might think you're gay.

Several respondents specifically listed "The Kama Sutra" as a book that should not be on a bookshelf. Apparently, they want us to read it, but they don't want to see it.

If you have a life-sized cardboard cutout of the Bud Girl or Carmen Electra or any other woman, please consider throwing it out in someone else's trash down the block; at the very least, you need to stash it in the way back of the closet. As for male cardboard cutouts, my friend Denis grew up adoring Dan Marino. He – Denis, not Dan – had a life-sized cutout of #13 in uniform standing guard in his TV room all throughout his twenties. Amazingly, he got married nine years ago. Even more amazing, Denis still has Dandy Dan standing guard in his TV room and is still married.

Regardless, I do not recommend such risk taking.

On the topic of <u>risky</u>, find and hide any recent packets of photos, i.e. anything you ordered from Ofoto, Snapfish, etc.

Ms. Right Now's natural feline curiosity will force her to flip through any and all pictures she finds. This could become problematic if you have shots of you and your ex, time stamped three weeks ago.

I paid the price for such foolishness in early 1998. I was "hanging out" with one woman, but went to Mexico with a different chick and three other couples. Upon my return I invited Girl #1 over for some fun. While I was in the kitchen grabbing drinks, she browsed through the just-back-from-the-photo-shop packets I left on the coffee table and saw several group shots in which I was always standing next to Girl #2. Nancy Drew put two and two together and stormed out before I could even begin my lame excuse.

Do yourself a favor and go one step further with your photo vigilance: download all the digital pics from your camera to your computer and then delete them from the camera.

You need some tunes to inspire your cleaning, brother. Crank it up.

And that reminds me, what's in your iPod for mood music during dinner? Contrary to what Damone tells Rat in "Fast Times at Ridgemont High," side two of Zeppelin IV will not get the job done. I suggest a rotation of five CDs: Sinatra's Greatest Hits Volumes 1&2 (what girl doesn't swoon for Frank?), Billie Holiday's anything (every girl knows Billie sings the blues, and her voice will knock more than your socks off), anything by Michael Buble (the newest Frank, his last name is pronounced – no shit – Boob-lay), anything by The Postal Service or Snow Patrol, and Miles Davis's Blue (the hep-est cat in jazz).

Take everything off your TV.

Spray it down with Glass Plus, and wipe it off with the paper towels. Now, you've gotta clean *inside* the TV.

Turn it on. What channel comes on first? Better not be Skinemax. Make sure it's on something safe.

Now, go into the "saved recordings" section of your DVR. Are there any titles you might not want her to see? This is a major flaw in the DVR system, in that you can't change the title to something she'd never click on out of curiosity, like, "Tanks of World War II." If a strip club can make its credit card charge appear as "Joe's Diner," then the whiz kids who created DVR should be able to come up with a way to let us hide our shady movies.

Regardless, you gotta delete 'em. Don't worry; "Coed Confidential" will be on again real soon.

Speaking of movies, how's your DVD collection, classy guy? I'm thinking there's an inversely proportional ratio between Girls Gone Wild Turner Classic Movies.

I'm not suggesting you throw out your "fun" videos; I just want you to hide them with your porn and Preparation H. I do suggest, however, that you purchase five bonafide classics, preferably ones with a love story.

For example, "Casablanca" (in every critic's top 3 all-time movies, plus Bogey and great dialogue), "The Philadelphia Story," (don't let the stupid name fool you; rapid fire banter plus Cary Grant and Jimmy Stewart chasing the same girl), "On The Waterfront," (Brando. Boxing. Love story), "The Hustler" (Paul Newman shoots pool, gets girl), and "From Here to Eternity" (a million times the movie "Pearl Harbor" tried to be, plus Sinatra in his Oscar winning role). For modern romantic comedies, you can't go wrong with these three: "Moonstruck" (Cher is gorgeous – no, really – and Nic Cage is loony), "When Harry Met Sally" (if you get cable you've seen this a million times) and "Say Anything" (read Chuck Klosterman's essay on how every girl in America wants to bang John Cusack).

And if you don't feel like buying the movies, you can always rent them from Netflix. (But you'll have to re-rent them if she ever comes back for a second date.)

You're not done with the TV, just yet. Are the controllers to your PSP/X-Box stretched across the room so they can reach the couch?

Not anymore they're not. You don't have to roll them up, but you gotta put 'em away.

Speaking of the couch, pull off all the cushions. This is more than a task designed to find you enough change to pay for the Sunday paper; this is a preemptive strike.

Let's say dinner goes well, really well, and you and Ms. Right Now end up rolling around on the couch. In the heat of the moment, jerseys and sofa cushions go flying. She sticks out a hand to brace herself, but ends up with Frito crumbs stuck to her palm. I can practically hear the sound of Yoda dying.

Grab the vacuum, and clean up the exposed couch. Replace the pillows and prop them up all nice-like.

Then, grab the Febreze and lightly mist the cushions; not that I think your couch might need some anti-microbials or anything.

If you're a future lung cancer patient, I mean, Smoker, move every ashtray to the deck or fire escape. I know, I know: it's your castle and you can do whatever you want inside it. With that attitude, Prince Charming, you're not getting laid tonight or any time soon. Your princess will not appreciate a pile of butts stinking up the joint. Move 'em.

If you're a future lip cancer patient, I mean, Dipper, scour the apartment for the 17 forgotten Mountain Dew bottles half-filled with your brown spit. Recycle those Skoal Cocktails, and immediately take the trash outside before you have a Category 3 Haz Mat situation on your hands.

Your bong. If you already know she sparks up, it probably doesn't matter where you keep it, though the dining room table might be a bit much.

If you don't know, play it safe and stick it in the closet.

You can always pull out the weed after the topic comes up. Cocaine-dusted mirrors or heroin kits should probably remain hidden until she says something like, "Who do I have to blow around here to get a fix?"

I'm not sure where you maintain your home office – most guys have it in the living room or bedroom – so I'll just address this important area now.

You don't have to clear your desktop of mail, random papers, etc. But you do need to put them in some kind of order, indicating that you actually have "a system."

Most importantly, you don't want to leave visible any of the following: betting slips, "Past Due" bills, itemized hotel receipts with $25 all-day movie charges, or $30,000 Visa balances.

Ditto for restraining orders.

On the flip side, if you have a big fat paycheck you wouldn't mind her seeing, you might leave it "half hidden" on the desk; after all, the medicine cabinet isn't the only place she might snoop.

Whoa! Check your computer settings/internet history just as closely as you did for your TV! Delete all recent history that you wouldn't want your mom to see.

As a final desk requirement, use the rag to wipe down the lamp, stapler, paper clip dispenser, etc.

Find your magazine rack and place it beside a couch or between the couch and easy chair. Take every magazine currently on top of, inside or underneath your coffee table, and place them in the rack.

Haven't see the top of the coffee table in a while, eh?

Grab the Glass Plus and spray the top of the table, or whatever semi-flat object you've been using as a coffee table. Wipe it down with a paper towel. There may be some "stuff" on there that takes repeated sprayings and scrubbings.

Grab two candles and place them strategically around the living room. You don't often get to freelance, Private, so take advantage of the opportunity.

Dude, you are so almost done. Only floor duty remains.

If you have a hardwood floor, wield your Swiffer and pick up all that dust, sofa feathers, and chip crumbs. Then, unleash the Wet Swiffer and make that floor shine. Be careful not to back yourself into a corner.

If you have a rug, fire up that vacuum and do the same. Rug-guys, if you've had a party in the past two months, you might want to sprinkle some Carpet Fresh and re-vacuum. Not that anybody would ever spill a beer at a soiree of yours.

Drop a quarter on the floor. Watch it roll. Get down on all fours to pick it up.

While you're down there, take a look around: you might see something under the couch or TV stand or desk you missed earlier. Try the quarter thing a few more times; you'll be glad you did.

Make one last sweep of the living room, keeping a vigilant eye out for dirty paper towels and Swiffer cloths.

Admire your handiwork. But don't sit down!

BATHROOM

Needs: Glass Plus, Comet Bathroom Cleaner, Drano, Swiffer, Wet Swiffer, Swiffer pads both dry and wet, vacuum, old dishwashing sponge with Astroturf side, Q-tips, rags, paper towels, two new tooth brushes, toilet brush <u>and</u> toilet brush holder.

Before you do anything, open the window and hit the exhaust fan; you'll be using enough cleaning agents to sedate a kindergarten.

Once again, start at the top.

Grab the vacuum with the hose attachment. Look up at the corners. See any cobwebs? Perhaps not. This may be due to the fact that the upper walls are covered by one continuous web. Suck it away, sir!

Don't put down the vacuum hose just yet.

Turn off the bathroom fan, which, in my estimation, is the third greatest invention of the past 50 years, trailing only the television remote control and TiVo. Take a good look at the grate covering the fan. It's all gunked up, isn't it? Use the vacuum hose to free your friend from its dust shackles and let it do the job it was born to do.

Remember that Southwest Airlines commercial where the woman opens the guy's medicine cabinet and all the glass shelves fall out, totally busting her? Everyone laughs at that one because it's true; chicks are Super Snoopers. Rather than try to reverse millions of years of DNA encoding, just deal with it.

Open said medicine cabinet. Empty the shelves. Grab a damp rag and wipe them down. Next, wipe down everything that was on those shelves (saline solution cases, in particular, attract grime). Return everything to its rightful spot.

Uh, you might want to put the following items – in descending order of importance – someplace a little less public: Valtrex, Lithium, Viagra, Propecia, PreparationH, Compound W, and Beano.

You may want to leave your Xanax in there, since some chicks like a guy who's been to therapy. That's your call.

Speaking of Viagra, if you're still using Vitamin V instead of Cialis, you're missing out. A 36-hour "window of opportunity" beats the crap out of a 4-hour window. And since you're stealing the samples from your father's/uncle's/friend's medical practice, anyway, why not participate in a modern day Pepsi Challenge? See if you can tell the difference. You won't be disappointed.

Back to the medicine cabinet! Make sure you move your dental floss, toothpaste, and Flax to the first shelf, right at *female* eye level! Dental hygiene is way more important to women than it is to men; it's a little known fact that George Washington did not pull wool. It had to be the teeth, right? After all, he was the most powerful guy in the nation. Close the medicine cabinet.

Look in the mirror.

If your reflection is obscured by more than zero self-motivational Post-Its, remove each and every one of them immediately. Good God, are you insane, man? That's like hanging little "Here are the areas where I am most vulnerable and can be taken advantage of with the least effort!" signs. (Note: If you have any of these on the dashboard of your car, run outside and get rid of those, too.)

Look in the mirror again.

You probably don't see yourself very clearly. This is reminiscent of Joe Pesci's title character in "My Cousin Vinny," when he's cross-examining the witness. Vinny asks, "What's all this…<u>stuff</u>?" on the window screen. After a moment the hick hesitantly says, "Dirt?" Vinny smiles reassuringly and says, "That's right! Don't be afraid. Go ahead and shout it out!" So, you're staring at your mirror and you're thinking it's fairly clean. *Dude.* The girl who's coming over tonight could teach Gil Grissom and his CSI team a thing or two about finding incriminating evidence. She can tell when you switched from Colgate to Crest, and that you had an infected whitehead two Thanksgivings ago.

Grab the Glass Plus and drench that glass. Dry it with a paper towel in a consistent up and down motion.

Now, look down at the sink. Unfortunately, apartments often have poor drainage, allowing generations of dripped-off toothpaste and shaved whiskers to create barnacles in your sink. I understand this, and share your belief that there's no use in cleaning them off each time because their cousins will stick there eventually. Alas, the female species does not agree with you and I.

Turn on the hot water and, once it's scalding, plug the drain. When the sink is full, turn off the water and let it sit like that for a few minutes, hopefully softening up the crust.

Do twenty pushups. What, you don't want to be pumped up for your date?

Back to the sink. Unplug the drain. Drown the sink in Comet Bathroom Cleaner. Let it soak in for a moment.

Then, with Astroturf sponge in hand, start scrubbing as feverishly as you'd clean up the blood from a crime scene. Just saying.

If you have sink drainage issues, read this. If not, skip to the next paragraph. Grab the Drano and pour half the bottle down the sink. It needs to sit for 15 minutes.

Once the sink shines like the day you moved in, raise your line of sight to the basin (that's the area around the sink).

Remove your razor, shaving cream, toothpaste, etc. Spray the surface with Comet Bathroom Cleaner. Let that soak in before wiping the basin down.

Next, take your Glass Plus and drench the fixtures. Let it soak. Wiping these down will take some serious elbow grease, as they probably haven't been cleaned since Jack Bauer started having bad days.

Once that's done, lean toward the wall and peer down into the tiny gap between the faucet and the back of the basin. *Ick.* Grab a Q-tip and try to clean up as much of that gunk as possible. Do this several times.

Now, as with the medicine cabinet, you need to wipe down everything that was on the basin, paying particular attention to the crud on your Mach 3 holder and the dust on top of your shaving cream can top. (If you use an electric razor to trim your goatee or, like me, cut what hair you have left with clippers, make sure you look carefully for whiskers that have floated onto weird spots: the wall, the window sill, etc.)

The need to remove the shaving cream, razor and toothpaste reminds me of a painful lesson. After receiving a sudden job promotion to California, I put my home in Indiana on the market and left it in the questionable hands of my roommates. Despite a large number of showings, the realtor could not sell the house, jeopardizing the 2% of the sale price bonus I would have received from Pfizer as reward for saving the company the hassle of buying the house as part of my relocation deal. After one annoyed voice mail from the realtor mentioned, "The smell of wet dog," I decided to place a call to my roomies.

Steve shared a conversation he'd had with his then girlfriend, now wife, Michelle. After using the bathroom just hours after a couple had toured the house, she asked Steve, "So, you take your shaving cream and razor off the basin for the showing, and then put it back right after they leave?" Steve's clueless look said it all: he never once put away the toiletries before any the showings. I never did collect that 2% bonus.

Think of women as prospective homebuyers; they're not pulling the trigger when a can of Edge is rusting up the basin. Do yourself a favor, and store that stuff in the medicine cabinet or build a shelf.

Take a step back from the sink and look down at the other oval object in the bathroom. Yes, I hear the lambs still screaming, too. The toilet. Ugh.

Let's start off easy. Toilet paper. I don't care what brand you have or what thickness it is (though I am a two-ply man, myself). Just make sure you have enough of it. Remember, women use TP <u>every time</u> they go. Every time. You're gonna need a back up roll, brother. Also, spend the extra ten seconds it takes to place the roll on the actual toilet paper dispenser. This, by itself, will distinguish you from 95% of the guys she ever dated.

Remove everything from the top of tank, and wipe it down with a rag.

There are two theories to your magazine collection: 1) Hide the "Maxim," "FHM," and "Stuff;" she already thinks you're a shallow guy who likes to drool over women with fake boobs, but that doesn't mean you need to prove her right, or 2) Neatly place the aforementioned soft-core periodicals in a magazine rack; since she already knows you're a shallow guy who likes to drool over women with fake boobs, she'll be suspicious when she *doesn't* see those magazines in your bachelor pad. Of the women surveyed, a strong majority identified some sort of porn (to include, "Maxim," "FHM" and even the Victoria's Secret catalog!) as a deal breaker. You're on thin ice here, Gretzky. You make the call.

Pick up the five books of matches you have handy to override the occasional odoriferous offense, and throw out any obtained from a Gentleman's Club. Take the G-rated ones and place them in a nice, little bowl (chicks love their bowls). In fact, it's a good idea to buy a matching set of bathroom items (soft soap dispenser, waste basket, little bowl and toothbrush holder) at Bed, Bath and Beyond. Trust me, she won't think you're gay. But if you don't have time for that two-hour adventure to the store, simply find a bowl or glass jar for the matches as a stopgap measure.

With that lay-up under your belt, you're graduating to the tougher challenges.

For a good example of how to properly clean a toilet, rent "Singles." Pay close attention to Kyra Sedgwick's technique with her ex-boyfriend's T-shirt.

Bottom line: you gotta get down on your knees and scrub all the unintended targets you and your buddies have undoubtedly strafed with friendly fire.

Focus carefully on the run-off channels down the sides and the area beyond the "center field wall," as I like to call it.

Empty a few rounds of Comet into the toilet. You'll come back to this in a minute.

Take a rag or paper towel and wipe down the dusty underside of the toilet lid.

Next, lift up the toilet seat. See those brown stains? The Space Shuttle makes less of a splash upon reentry than you do the day after a 3 a.m. burrito.

Drench that bad boy in Comet Bathroom Cleaner and let it soak in. Saturate your old dishwashing sponge in the sink.

Now, grab your toilet brush and go to town on the toilet bowl. Be aggressive, as if you're grilling out and just dropped a $30 NY strip in the coals. Concentrate on the narrow bottom, and don't forget to jam the brush under the lip where the water comes out and "other stuff" sometimes hides.

Flush. It's easy to check your progress: lighter colored areas are better than darker areas. Keep scrubbing and flushing until the entire bowl is uniform in color (uniformly "yellowish" is not acceptable unless the top of the toilet tank is yellowish).

Rinse off the brush by sticking it under the clean water after a flush, and shake it off above the toilet before replacing it in its holster.

Back to the underside of the toilet seat, the cleaning equivalent of diving in front of a slap shot. Grab the wet sponge and flip it over so that the Astroturf side is the active one. Start scrubbing. Might not be a bad idea to take a page out of Michael Keaton's handbook from "Mr. Mom" and place a clothespin over your nose.

Once you've eradicated the incriminating evidence, wipe the bottom (no pun intended) and top of the seat with wet paper towels. Then, toss them and the sponge into the HazMat bin behind your place.

You should practice always putting down the toilet seat in your own home. This way, it will become second nature to you, eliminating the risk of leaving the seat up at her place and proving you are a selfish ogre.

My cousin Brian (former US Army Ranger, current "Green" guru), however, recommends the opposite course of action if you ever have to take a dump at those bars with the trendy unisex bathrooms.

Race in and drop the deuce as fast as possible, but leave the seat in the upright position afterward. When you exit, make a pained expression as you assure the chick on line that it was the guy in front of you who destroyed the place.

She won't believe you – smart girl – but when she sees the toilet seat in the upright position, she will realize that since you never sat down, you couldn't be the culprit.

And you'll still have a chance to cook for her the next weekend.

Morning After note: Once you've taken your Austin Powers piss in the a.m. grab some toilet paper and wipe up the floor in front of the toilet where her bare feet will rest when she uses the facilities. Splashing around first thing in the morning will not rev her engines for another lap around your bed.

Back to the now.

Turn the hot water on in the sink. Let it run for a minute, rinsing the Drano away.

At this point, you deserve a break. Grab a quick drink of water, flip on the TV to check out some scores, but whatever you do…don't sit down!

To paraphrase Vince Lombardi, "Cleaning the bathroom makes cowards of us all." It's way too easy to stay seated once you've schlumped down on your couch. Rally and stay focused. You need to finish what you've started – do the job right, George Herbert Bush, and steamroll all the way into Baghdad!

You know what you need to do to motivate yourself. If it's visualizing Drill Sergeant Louis Gossett, Jr. kicking you in the nads because your latrine wouldn't pass inspection, then think about that. Me? I'd be thinking how close I was to enticing Ms. Right Now into my shower.

Visualize her standing in your bathroom. The mirror shines, the sink gleams, the toilet sparkles. *Hmm, this guy cooks AND cleans! I may need to wash his balls later.* But the shower has to dazzle her before she puts Operation Soapy Soapy into motion.

You'll begin <u>outside</u> the shower.

I'm assuming you only own one bathmat. And you've had it since graduation. I'm also assuming that you do not have time to wash that old friend before she arrives.

Pick up the mat and fold it inward like you're a hobo who's about to tie it to a stick before hopping a freight train. Take the bathmat out back behind your place and – after closing your eyes and taking a deep breath – start shaking it out. Rest. Breathe. Repeat. Now, brush off the dust and pubes that have settled onto your shirt.

This is a good time for me to recommend purchasing a bath rug, or something more substantial than the glorified washcloths found in your old dorm's shower room. Preferably, this bathmat will match your collection of bath towels, which, in turn, will match the bathroom's color scheme. (Yeah, you definitely need to schedule a trip to Bed, Bath and Beyond, preferably chaperoned by a sister or gal pal.)

When it comes to towels, women think bigger is better. Investing in two "bath sheets" – the ones that can wrap her up several times over – is a good move.

Don't forget that girls use washcloths and those little towels that don't really have any purpose. Make sure you have those ready for sleepovers. Yes, those have to match, too. At an absolute minimum, they cannot have "Holiday Inn" printed on them.

Oh, yeah. I almost forgot. All the towels you put out MUST be clean.

I still can't believe it took me 38 freaking years to learn this next tip, but I will set aside my shame for your sake. Do not hang your shower towel near the shitter!!! All cloth absorbs odors; wet cloth traps them. Nothing like drying off with a towel that smells like the aforementioned damage from that 3 a.m. burrito.

Back to the decontamination.

I'm guessing that your shower curtain isn't fit to wrap a dead body in, let alone hang in your bathroom. If time is not an issue, pull it down, roll it up and throw it in the rapidly filling Hazmat bin. Then go buy a new one at BBB (Remember, it should jibe with the color concept you've got going. Also, clear shower curtains provide more light through the window, which could be a good thing or bad thing depending on the age and quality of your bathroom).

If you don't have time for that mission, step inside the shower and drench the curtain with Comet Bathroom Cleaner; at least that might kill some living organisms.

For those of you with glass shower doors, you gotta get one of those squeegee things and use it with Glass Plus. Seriously.

Remove everything from the shower. Liquid-wise, this should only include a bottle of shampoo, a bottle of conditioner, and a bottle of body wash, a.k.a. liquid soap.

Any exfoliating creams, tightening lotions, etc. should be thrown out on principle alone, but at the very least hidden. You don't want to have more stuff than she does, Guy. Tool-wise, you can have a scrub brush and a washcloth – that's it. You absolutely cannot have one of those nylon thingies that looks like a jellyfish!

Your goal for the shower is to make it clean enough to wash vegetables a la Kramer; not that any of the meals in this book will require you to do so, however.

Like with everything else, start at the highest point and work your way down.

Take a look at the showerhead. If you see anything other than air in the holes, you need to blast it with cleaner and scrub like crazy. Hello, mold.

Stand back and stare at your shower walls. See any dark spots? Dude, you've been hosting a botany experiment, and you didn't even know it. Chicks can sense mold spots with the lights turned off, like a disturbance in The Force. Fortunately, correcting your mold problem is easy. Sadly, it takes a lot of elbow grease. Douse the walls with Comet cleaner, and let it soak in for a few minutes. Do some arm stretches. Then, grab your sponge and start scrubbing.

Regardless of whether you store the bar of soap in the built-in wall slot or on a rack hanging from the showerhead, you will need to clean the soap dish. For real. How many dead soldiers do you have piled up like melted candles? I'm guessing at least three. While I respect your adherence to military code – "Never leave your dead!" – Ms. Right Now will definitely not appreciate the art project gone bad.

Scrape off the lumpy, hard ball of soap and throw it out. Next, scrub the dish, so no remnants remain. Do the same thing to the trail of soap that has dripped down the wall and hardened.

Look down at your feet. Try not to scream. Probably not necessary for me to tell you what to do, but just to be sure: get down on your knees and start scrubbing.

(Note: one of those rubber, no-slip mats is a great way to cover up a dirty shower floor. Plus, she'll think safety's important to you. "Safety" naturally triggers thoughts of "safe sex," which may lead to her thinking, "I want to rail him tonight!" However, a dirty rubber mat may be grosser than the dirty tub floor the former is supposed to hide, which would defeat the purpose entirely.)

The drip area below the faucet is undoubtedly discolored, probably indelibly from hard water; but since you're already down on your knees, give it a good scrub. For the team.

In that same area of operation, examine the drain. *Psst*. It's underneath the pound of matted hair. Might wanna remove that human Brillo pad.

Big apartment complexes often have drainage problems of their own; if you live in one, do yourself a favor and pre-emptively use the rest of the Draino. Standing ankle deep in scummy water is not going to entice your angel to invite you in for the aforementioned soapy soapy.

Now, run the hot water and wash down every surface in the shower.

"They're coming down the homestretch..."

Fellas, we are hairy bastards. Grab the Swiffer (or the vacuum with the hose attachment) and keep Swiffing until the floor no longer resembles a barbershop at closing time. Next, have fun with the wet Swiffer – the spray mechanism is a blast – and make that floor shine, Private Joker. Take the seven used Swiffer pads out to the Haz Mat bin.

Your last chore is done under the assumption that your efforts will be rewarded.

If Ms. Right Now spends the night, she will more than likely want to brush her teeth – especially in the morning. If you have a case of toothbrushes at her disposal, though, she might think you're a bit too prepared for sleepovers. Since dentists recommend replacing your toothbrush every three months, having one or two on hand isn't a sign of promiscuity, but oral sensibility.

Place the new toothbrushes in the medicine cabinet or in a bin under the sink.

As the ugly gal pal in "Say Anything" told John Cusack, "Get ready for greatness, Lloyd!"

BEDROOM

NEEDS: Vacuum cleaner with hose attachment, Glass Plus, paper towels, clean sheets, candle, Kleenex, clothes hamper

The bedroom is like the Red Zone in a football game, isn't it? The Steelers spend all this money (on players), time (strategizing) and energy (training and practicing) to score inside the 20-yard line.

Team You spends all this money (on food and beverages), time (acquiring the necessities) and energy (cleaning) to score in the bedroom.

As usual, you're starting high and working your way down. Cobweb duty all around the room. Those with a ceiling fan, you know what to do.

If you have mirrors on the ceiling, I salute you, sir! And I suggest you come up with an explanation for their presence in your home, preferably something involving the previous tenants being abusive foster parents from whom you rescued their tortured kids.

If you live in one of those massive two-story apartment complexes in which every bedroom is festooned with mirrored closet doors, you don't need an explanation. You do, however, need to make sure they are free of any fingerprints and "smudges."

Grab the Glass Plus and a paper towel and get to work.

Take a gander at your walls. Chicks dig framed prints of French lighthouses, French train stations and French paintings. Just like in the living room, beer posters are not allowed, but neither are neon beer signs.

Wipe everything down with paper towels and Glass Plus.

Remove everything from the top of your dresser. *What's that? You use milk crates to store your clothes?* If you are under 25, that is permissible. If older than 25, they've invented this place called Ikea. Go there. Immediately.

Wipe off the top of the dresser.

You're not done with the Glass Plus or paper towels. Move over to your nightstand – you do have a nightstand, right? If not, get one STAT.

Remove everything from the nightstand. Spray down the dustbowl and wipe it clean. Now, wipe the lamp off and put it back in place. Dust off the lampshade. Wipe the clock down and put it back where it belongs.

Grab the candle and place it on the outside corner where its flame will be maximized. Now, light it; I don't want it to burn so much that it appears you've had a hundred girls sleep over, but I also don't want the wick looking brand new, as if you just busted out the candle today to try and impress her. Which you did.

Now, place a book on the table. Which book isn't important, but the fact that it is being read is. For a hardcover, open it, take out the front jacket flap, and place it between two random pages; with a paperback, leave it standing in a V, so that the spine is stretched.

It'd be smart to actually read the pages to which you've opened the book, just in case she administers a Pop Quiz. Teacher always did like the bright kids!

A picture of your family or a non-vulgar one of your buddies is a nice touch.

There's just one thing left on the nightstand. Let's say Ms. Right Now sneezes during the night. What are you going to hand her to soak up the snot at that increasingly awkward moment? Toilet paper ain't gonna cut it.

Open the Kleenex box and place it on top, if there's room, or underneath if there isn't. Blow out the candle.

If you have a TV in your bedroom, repeat the cleaning steps from the living room – outside <u>and</u> inside the TV.

Also, make sure to check the VCR/DVD player for porn. The latter may seem unnecessary to mention, but I've got a friend who left in a "Blacks on Blondes" video; he thought he'd already switched it out for – no shit – "Dumb and Dumber." Can't ever be too careful.

Finally, you've reached the Promised Land: bed. Don't fumble on the goal line, Bettis!

This is a good time to mention that several women surveyed had major problems with men who still own stuffed animals. Something to think about…

When people walk into a bedroom, the first thing they naturally look at is the bed. This fact makes the comforter the most important object in the room. Have you ever seen an unattractive hostess at a hip restaurant? Didn't think so. Your comforter, like a hostess, represents the entire organization.

With that possibly frightening thought in mind, I've got a mental exercise for you: think of how old you were when you got that comforter, and who paid for it.

If the answers are "Five or more years younger than I am now" and/or "Mom," it's probably time for a new comforter. If *you* bought it *less* than five years ago, but it has those fuzzy fabric balls sticking to it, it's probably time for a new comforter.

If you don't have time to run to Bed, Bath and Beyond before Ms. Right Now arrives, though, add this to your to-buy list and drop the old guy off at the dry cleaner's. If you don't even have enough time for that, hang it outside for 30 minutes.

If hanging it outside is not an option, spray the comforter with a dash of Febreze and then flip it over to its less fabric ball-y side.

Lift off the comforter; take a good look at the sheets. Think for a moment. If you did not just put them on the bed yesterday, immediately rip them off.

Clean sheets are an absolute must! But comfort is important, too. Women love to luxuriate in bed – so the higher the thread count, the better off you are.

Thread count is the number of horizontal and vertical threads in one square inch of fabric, and the number can range from 80 to 700. Most stores sell sheets that range from 180 to 320. In general, the higher the thread count, the softer the fabric will feel on her skin. For your purposes, anything over 300 will be rewarded.

"Pillows? Those aren't pillows!" I'm guessing you or your mother bought your pillows along with the comforter. People are quite particular about their pillows – just ask Steve Martin's character – so I'm not going to advise you on fluffy, firm, etc. I will say that comparisons to sleepaway camp pillows are not a good thing.

Remember to throw the pillowcases in with the sheets when you wash them.

Having remade the bed, now drop down to the floor. Take a long look underneath the bed and dresser. Anything there you don't want her to see, like empty condom wrappers, used Kleenex or "Swank?"

Remove any evidence you discover. Obviously, your crusty cum-towel will have to be relocated for the evening.

Stand up and look all around the floor. See any wayward jeans or T-shirts?

In a pinch you can always use the traditional last resort of throwing all the dirty clothes into the closet, but that's risky. But what if our super snooper expands her search parameters outside the medicine cabinet?

You really need some type of receptacle in which to place your laundry. Whether it's a $40 tri-plex from Target that lets you isolate the clothes by colors, or simply two plastic wash-baskets (Because it's important to show her you know that reds don't go with whites, you need more than one hamper-like thing), you'll be okay.

If you wear thongs or Manties (think John Travolta in "Saturday Night Fever") bury them at the bottom of the pile.

Having picked up your clothes from the floor, take a look at that flat space you probably haven't seen in a while.

You should know the drill by now: Swiffer for hardwood, or the vacuum for carpet. Make sure you get all the hairballs beneath the bed and dresser, too.

Now ask yourself: if you were a woman, would you want to find out how your clothes look on the floor?

If the answer is "yes," then you are set to go, sir!

PART THREE: DUDE

PRE-FLIGHT CHECKLIST

A pilot runs through a specific checklist prior to each flight; he does it in the same sequence, the same way every time. While you may not be a fighter jock looking to successfully pull a 9g turn before going to guns, you <u>are</u> looking to pull an overnight guest onto your jock before successfully firing your gun.

You, then, also need a pre-flight checklist.

But in this case, you are both aviator and aircraft. And everything has to be perfect prior to taxiing onto the runway.

Don't think of yourself as Maverick. You are Ice Man. You are thorough, precise and you never make a mistake. (Besides, you'd never play beach volleyball in your jeans, and Val Kilmer is, like, a million times cooler than Tom Cruise now, anyway.)

PRE-SHOWER

Weapons: Tiny scissors, tweezers, dry razor, Q-tips

Just like when cleaning the apartment, we're going to start at the top and work our way down.

__ **Eyebrows**. If you stare in the mirror and notice an uncanny resemblance to your Uncle Walter that was not there three months ago, you need to grab the scissors and start hacking away at those runaway brows.

__ **Nose hairs**. Ah, ah, ah! Not so fast. Before you start peeking into those stalactite-lined caves you call nostrils, take a close look at the top and outsides of your actual nose. Chances are you'll find some rogue hairs. Tweeze away, fella. Next, take those scissors and start chopping away inside the nostrils. Keep in mind: Ms. Right Now is probably shorter than you. This means she will have a steeper sightline into your nasal nests. Tilt your head back and take a second look from a different angle. Snip, snip.

__ **Ears**. Like an ambidextrous coal miner, arm yourself with Q-tips and go drilling. Repeat with clean swabs until the tips emerge from your ears still white. (Note: For those older than 35, you are a 2:1 shot for ear hair. Snip, snip. Sob, sob.)

__ **Neck**. Take a dry razor and lightly clean up the whiskers that have sprung up like wild flowers on the sides of your neck from your ears down to your traps (I'm giving you the benefit of the doubt that you do, in fact, have trapezius muscles). Next, run your hand over the back of your neck. Feel anything furry? Hmm, that's what my old roommate called an "Ass Neck." Sounds like a deal breaker to me. Cleaning up this crucial area may require you to seek outside help. In a pinch, take the dry razor and lightly run it down your neck. Periodically duck into the shower and blow on the razor to unclog it; this way, no hairs hit the bathroom floor.

__ **Upper back and shoulders**. Twist your upper torso both way to check for Backne. Women don't want to run their fingernails over your skin and rip the top off a whitehead. If you find 'em, pop 'em. Please resist the teenager within you screaming, "Hit the mirror! Hit the mirror!" You just cleaned that glass, remember? Remember to get some soap on that open wound once you're in the shower.

__ **Big Jim and the Twins**. I don't care if you Manscape or if you don't. But she might.

__ **Rub one out**. Like the guy says in "Something About Mary," you can't go on a date with a loaded gun in your pocket.

IN SHOWER

___ If you didn't dry clean your shirt and you can't/won't iron, then hang it in the bathroom while you're in the shower. Crank the hot water. The steam should help with the wrinkles. And then go buy some carbon emissions credits.

___ Do <u>not</u> pee in the shower. You just spent twenty minutes scrubbing that floor! Eau de Piss is not the scent she wants to find in the bathroom.

___ Blow your nose. Hard. Gotta clear out any hangers.

___ Aim the showerhead all over the place to make sure you wash away all the snot, dead pubes, etc.

POST-SHOWER

Weapons: Visine, nail clippers

__ **Eyes**. After spending hours in a haze of dust mites and cleaning solutions, your eyes probably resemble road maps. Grab some Visine and get the red out.

__ **Beard**. You're shaving twice tonight, Mariano. Shave down, then rinse and shave upwards. You want to be smoother than the bikini waxing you hope she just got.

__ Even up your sideburns; you don't want one up in Atlanta and one down in Miami.

__ Be sure to check the area below your Adam's Apple for wily whiskers.

__ **Fingernails**. You don't want to remind her of Wolverine. Also, clip off any hang nails or damaged cuticles. That sounds gayer than it is.

__ **Toenails**. Do your toenails resemble Jeff Daniels's in "Dumb and Dumber?" Even worse, do they look like your Dad's? Take advantage of the fact they've been softened by the shower's hot water; trim those bad boys down to a length TSA would allow on a domestic flight.

__ **Cologne**. A little is too much. On a trip home to my parents' house, I once applied a "dash" of Nautica Sport to my wrists and then rubbed my neck. My sister, sitting in the dining room, exclaimed, "Whoa!" before I'd even entered the kitchen. *Bon voyage, Nautica*. And, despite what the commercials claim, chicks hate Axe; they know you're only using it because you saw the guy have a threesome at the super market. Chuck it.

POST-DRESSING

__ Check to make sure you're wearing a belt. Seems silly, but lots of guys forget it – Jerry Seinfeld went two seasons without wearing one. Your belt should match your shoes. Under no circumstances are you allowed to wear a brown weave belt.

__ If you ignored the earlier advice on steaming your shirt, it might have annoying bumps on the shoulders from being on the hanger a long time. These are easy to remove – without an iron! Simply wet your fingertips with water, and pat down the bumps. Get them fairly damp. As the bumps dry out, they will vanish.

__ Set your cell phone set to "vibrate." You don't want it ringing all through dinner, especially if it's the other woman calling repeatedly. If you end up making out on the couch – Atta, baby! – reset the phone to silent, so she can't feel the vibrations through your pants pocket.

__ If you're the last guy in America who still uses an answering machine on your home phone, stop. Nothing good can come of that. Switch to voice mail, already! For tonight, though, at the very least turn down the volume to zero, so she can't hear the messages left by the aforementioned stalker.

AFTERWORD

So I've only got one more piece of advice for you: <u>relax</u>.

You're gonna be nervous the first few times you cook, even if you're only fixing something for yourself. Don't sweat those annoying butterflies; they're normal.

Thankfully, the more often you cook, the more familiar you'll get with the tools. The more familiar you get with the tools, the easier it'll get. The easier it gets, the more fun you'll have.

Just liking taking off a girl's bra. Remember your first time? Nerves and a lack of familiarity with the equipment led to near disaster. But after a few more opportunities, you got the hang of it. Pretty soon you were like a soldier disassembling his M-16 blindfolded.

So relax. After you cook for Ms. Right Now, her bra is gonna look great on your freshly cleaned floor.

ACKNOWLEDGMENTS

On July 4, 2006, Tim Meade approached me at a barbeque with an idea for a book. Since I was dating his very attractive sister Kat at the time – and wanted to continue dating her – I would've agreed to co-write anything. Fortunately, Tim had a funny concept. Unfortunately, he didn't have the free time to work on the project with me. After many permutations, I created "Bachelor 101." Thanks, Kat, for keeping me around long enough to meet your brother. And thanks, Tim, for the seed that germinated into this book.

Chef David Lefevre provided seasoning tips and advice on preparing red meat. He also throws an annual "Champagne & Oysters" party that is killer.

Jeff Jacobsen, Eric Vitale and U.S. Army captain Sean Murphy squared me away as far as the utensils and pots and pans every cook must have. All three guys also provided me with some helpful tips and tricks in the kitchen.

Mike Simms made the wine recommendations for each entrée. Getting wine recommendations requires lots of wine drinking, by the way.

Josh Kagan gave me invaluable legal advice regarding the slippery slopes of culinary law.

You would not be reading this book without the sacrifices made by the insane women who let me cook for them. (Last names have been omitted to protect their good names!) Nat, Jaylynn, Kristy, Miranda, Jen and Marisa…THANKS!

Lastly, I need to thank those whose recipes I failed to successfully cook. I am sorry my culinary incompetence let you down. Take solace in the fact that not even my Mom got a recipe in the book! This illustrious roster includes: Lisa Callamaro, Bhanu Calvert, John Dalton, Colleen Pana, Kevin Rigney, Christine Rogers, DeShane Roppo, Gina Rothwell, Keri Simms, Syllene Solis, Erin Swanson, Sherrie Walters and Diane Zeolla.

www.ingramcontent.com/pod-product-compliance
Lightning Source LLC
Chambersburg PA
CBHW081013040426

42444CB00014B/3192